TWAYNE'S WORLD AUTHORS SERIES

A Survey of the World's Literature

Sylvia E. Bowman, Indiana University

GENERAL EDITOR

RUSSIA

Charles A. Moser, The George Washington University

EDITOR

Vasily Zhukovsky

TWAS 271

Vasily Zhukovsky

VASILY ZHUKOVSKY

By IRINA M. SEMENKO

Academy of the Sciences of the U.S.S.R.

TWAYNE PUBLISHERS

A DIVISION OF G. K. HALL & CO., BOSTON

Library of Congress Cataloging in Publication Data
Semenko, Irina Mikhailovna.
  Vasily Zhukovsky.

  (Twayne's world authors series; TWAS 271: Russia)
  Bibliography: p. 163–64.
  Includes index.
  1. Zhukovskiĭ, Vasiliĭ Andreevich, 1783–1852—
Criticism and interpretation.
PG3447.Z5Z874   891.7′1′3   75–23419
ISBN 0–8057–2995–X

Contents

About the Author

Irina Semenko (the daughter of the Ukranian poet Mikhail Semenko) is a specialist in the history of Russian lyric verse. She has taken part in preparing the text and commentaries for scholarly editions of Pushkin and Zhukovsky and is the author of numerous learned articles on the work of Pushkin, Zhukovsky, Baratynsky, Mandel'shtam. She has also published studies of the novels of two Soviet writers: Olga Forsch and Yuriy Tynyanov. She is the author of the book *Poets of the Pushkin Epoch,* published in Moscow, 1970.

Preface

In comparison with other European literatures, Russian lyric poetry
was late in maturing. This tardiness was the result of the particular
characteristics of Russian history and the hegemony of antiquated
forms that continued to dominate Russian literature up to the early
eighteenth century. After the Petrine reforms had transformed the
cultural life of the country by making possible extensive contacts
with Europe, Russian secular literature began developing with
extraordinary rapidity.

The development of Russian poetry can be divided into two
distinct stages. The first stage is linked with Mikhail Lomonosov and
Gavriil Derzhavin. Lomonosov was the creator of Russian secular
literary language, particularly the new "high" style. It was
Derzhavin—the first great Russian poet and Alexandr Pushkin's
mentor—who continued Lomonosov's work.

In the eighteenth century, the principal purpose of poetry was to
assist in enhancing the image of the state and in establishing civil
order; for this reason, the dominant note was naturally one of civil
"eloquence":

> Although tender passion
> Is no stranger to my heart,
> My chief enthusiasm
> Is for the hero's part.[1]

Thus wrote Lomonosov in his poem "A Conversation with Anac-
reon."

Poets perceived man's "inner world" as a world of "private" interests quite devoid of social significance. The dominating genre in
the poetry of this period was the ode, whose "high" style
Lomonosov and Derzhavin developed to perfection.

However, the growing awareness throughout Europe of the value of individual, personal thoughts and feelings led Russian literature toward a new reform. In Derzhavin's poetry we already find a mounting interest in people's private lives—their everyday lives, their loves. Accordingly, he began to adapt the poetic language created by Lomonosov, introducing a more conversational tone, but for a specific effect, for Derzhavin still conceived of man's intellectual life as being divided into two separate spheres: the "civic" and the "personal."

The second significant change in Russian literature took place at the turn of the century, and is associated with the Karamzinian reform. Nikolay Karamzin—and after him, Konstantin Batyushkov, but expecially Zhukovsky—reoriented poetry toward the disclosure of the inner world of the individual. The life of the soul gradually became widely conceived of as a harmonious combination of the sentiments on the one hand, and the philosophic, civic, and religious thoughts of the individual on the other. "Everything for the soul," Karamzin proclaimed. This trend set Russian literature on a far-reaching course: it was the birth of lyric poetry, with its specific perspectives of synthesizing the complex expression of man's awareness of himself and of the world about him.

Lyric poetry was not invested with hitherto unattainable possibilities; it touched upon fundamental questions of human life.

At the beginning of the nineteenth century, the ode gave way to the elegy. Readers and critics alike were undergoing a reversal of their attitudes toward the ode, not only because of its lack of psychological profundity but also because of the inhibitory conventionality of its emotional tone. The conflict between ode and elegy in Russian literature was in part a by-product of the conflict between classicism and romanticism. The elegy, a preromantic genre, was more adaptable to the new mood than the ode. Later, the odic style was to be used again by Pushkin, Evgeny Baratynsky, and Fyodor Tyutchev. Questions of poetic structure, however, proved to be the decisive factor. The elegy, steadily broadening the range of thought and emotion, gradually freed itself of the canonic features of the genre and was transmuted into a free lyric form.

The content of lyric poetry, too, could express a new profundity of thought and feeling as a result of serious semantic and stylistic work on language, and also because of the concomitant enrichment of the range of meanings.

Conversational words, when used in the new setting of the elegy, acquired an intensified aura of emotion and significance. The elegiac school strove to use words in such a way as to express a conception of the "feeling of the heart" as a real and far from straightforward complex of experience. This effort explains why the school relied to such a degree on "conversational," albeit "poeticized," harmonious language, and shrank with such repugnance, frequently exaggerated, from all coarseness of expression. Elegance and gracefulness were the characteristic features of the new lyrical style.

The part played by Zhukovsky in the creation of the new elegy was particularly significant. Karamzin wrote little poetry. His great contribution was in prose. As for Konstantin Batyushkov, Zhukovsky's friend and ally, his principal achievement lay in the genre of the love elegy. Zhukovsky was the first to give intimate lyric poetry a profound, all-embracing sense, and Pushkin valued him as a poet of "varied and powerful" style. These were qualities Pushkin himself was to inherit from Zhukovsky, and it was not without reason that he regarded himself as the pupil of the older poet.

"Without Zhukovsky, we would not have had a Pushkin," noted a younger contemporary of both poets, the critic Vissarion Belinsky. He also made the penetrating remark that it was Zhukovsky who gave Russian lyric poetry "the possibility of content."[2]

The individual quality of Zhukovsky's poetry is influenced by the fact that more than half of his work consists of translations. These translations were of great importance for the development of Russian literature, an importance transcending the purely cognitive. The majority of Zhukovsky's translations, particularly his lyric translations, are free adaptations. Zhukovsky would borrow a lyric subject and rework it stylistically in his own way. He himself wrote that "in prose, the translator is a slave; in verse, the translator is a rival who, having absorbed the ideal which—as he understands it—the author of the original was striving to achieve, transforms it, so to speak, into a creation of his own imagination."[3] Everything Zhukovsky touched assumed features of a lofty dreaminess, lyricism, and melodious tenderness. It is as though he were not simply translating from one language into another, but from one system of images into another. Western European themes and subjects are organically woven into the fabric of Russian poetry, enriching its spiritual content. There was nothing mechanical about this borrowing from others; each subject was felt as intensely as if it were the poet's own. Thus, Zhukovsky became one of the exponents of an important and characteristic feature of modern Russian culture.

In his ballads, Zhukovsky introduced his contemporaries to the themes of the ancient world and medieval chivalry. After he had reached full poetic maturity, Zhukovsky followed Nikolay Gnedich as one of the finest poetic translators of the Homeric epos, making these foreign themes an inalienable part of the heritage of Russian readers. It was Zhukovsky who gave Russian poetry its romantic conception of the East, in particular, of India, through his adaptations of Thomas Moore's *Lalla Rookh,* and other works. And by his translations (from the German) of genuine Indian tales from the *Mahabharata,* he was the first to acquaint Russian readers with Indian epic poetry.

Zhukovsky's influence as a translator was very far-reaching. Goethe, Schiller, Byron, Scott, Uhland, Southey, Stilling, the brothers Grimm, and many other western European poets and writers were made available to wide circles of Russian society through his efforts.

Zhukovsky's work, with its wide range of themes, opened up new horizons for the reading public of Russia and for Russian poetry.

Chronology

1818	Publication of verse collection *Für wenige*.
	Publication of second edition of *The Poetry of Vasily Zhukovsky*, parts I–III, and part IV, *Experiments in Prose*.
1821	Travels to Germany in retinue of Grand Duchess Alexandra Fyodorovna.
	Translation of Schiller's tragedy *The Maid of Orleans*.
1821–1822	Translates Byron's *The Prisoner of Chillon*.
1824	Publication of third edition of *The Poetry of Vasily Zhukovsky*, vols. I–III.
1826	Assumes duties of tutor to heir to the throne.
1828	First translations of extracts from *Iliad*.
1831	Summer in Tsarskoe Selo with Pushkin and Gogol.
	Publication of *Ballads and Tales by V. A. Zhukovsky*, parts I–II; also published in one volume.
1831–1836	Works on Russian version of Friedrich de la Motte-Fouqué's *Undine*.
1837–1839	Extended tour of Russia and western Europe with heir to the throne.
1837–1841	Translation of the legend of Nâla and Damayânti.
1841	Retirement from service at court.
1835–1844	Publication of fourth edition of *The Poetry of Vasily Zhukovsky*, vols. I–IX.
1842–1848	Translation of *Odyssey*.
1846–1847	Translation of legend of Rustem and Zorab.
1849	Publication of nine volumes of fifth (13-volume) edition of *The Poetry of Vasily Zhukovsky*.
1849–1850	Translation of two songs from *The Iliad*.
1852	April 12 (old style). Death of Vasily Zhukovsky in Baden-Baden.

CHAPTER 1

Life and Work

I Family and Upbringing

PERSONAL experience is the keynote of Zhukovsky's poetry. A very sensitive, gifted child, he was born on January 29, 1783, to Afanasy Ivanovich Bunin, a self-indulgent Russian aristocrat and landowner from the province of Tula, and a Turkish woman, given the Russian name Elizaveta Dementevna, who had been captured in 1770 at the taking of the fortress of Bendery and brought to Russia as a slave.

His mother's sister had been taken captive at the same time as Zhukovsky's mother, but she did not live very long. Consequently, Zhukovsky had relatives only on his father's side, who did all they could to suppress the facts of the awkward position in which the future poet had been placed by the very fact of his birth. It was, therefore, a great shock to the boy when he was finally told the truth of his origins.

Bunin's wife, Mariya Grigorevna, was the family member who suffered most from this event. Having lost several daughters and her only son, she now lost her husband, who had moved to an annex of the great house with Elizaveta Dementevna. They had three daughters, all of whom died young and, finally, a son.

There was a family legend to the effect that it was the birth of this son that effected a reconciliation among all three parties concerned. Mariya Grigorevna considered it her Christian duty to take the newborn baby under her protection. As a practical matter, he was adopted by the entire Bunin family, and for some time he continued to grow up as a carefree child, beloved by all. He was not given the family name of Bunin, however, but rather that of his godfather, a poor nobleman, Andrey Zhukovsky, who lived on the Bunin estate of "Mishenskoe." The future poet was not condemned to share the lot of the serfs, as were the illegitimate children of so many land-

owners, but he was destined to bring lasting fame to the noble name
that he had received in so curious a way.

Elizaveta Dementevna became deeply devoted to the mistress of
the estate, who had accepted and made much of her son, and was
even prepared tó renounce her rights as a mother. Indeed, over a
period of several years, the growing child came to think of Mariya
Grigorevna Bunina as his real mother.

Even after everything had been explained to the boy, there was
no change in the situation. The formal and practical aspects of the
family's relationships continued as before. His real mother, now the
housekeeper, did not have the right to sit down in the presence of
the lady of the manor, who continued to act as if she were his
mother; and, to add to the confusion, he called the Bunins'
daughter—his half-sister—*mamen'ka* ("mommy") until he was almost a grown youth.

Nor did the boy's situation change after Bunin's death in 1791.
Officially, he had been left nothing in his father's will, but Mariya
Grigorevna had promised her husband on his deathbed that she
would never part with Elizaveta Dementevna and would bring up
Vasily as her own son. She kept her promise and was always gentle
and affectionate toward the child, but he was aware of the peculiar
nature of his position and quietly suffered because of it. Later,
Zhukovsky was to note in his diaries the often-quoted lines: "I
formed the habit of keeping myself to myself, because no one was
particularly concerned for me and because all manifestations of
concern seemed to me to stem from charity."[1]

These first childhood impressions served to develop a certain
fatalism in Zhukovsky's character and to foster thoughts on the
ephemeral nature of the social make-up of the "soul." It is also
revealing that Zhukovsky was never indifferent to questions of law
and legitimacy in their broadest sense. The circumstances of his own
birth and childhood were not such as to encourage personal protest
or rebellion. While there have been those whose illegitimate origin
provided them the impetus toward protesting their status,
Zhukovsky was not one of them; on the contrary, he was impressed
by legitimacy: "No one is more attached to law and order than I
am," said the poet. This conviction was to play a decisive role in his
whole development.

Zhukovsky's earliest extant verses are presumed to have been
written when he was seven or eight years old. At the age of twelve,

the poet wrote a "historical" tragedy which has also survived—a tragedy in the pseudoclassical style of the day, entiled: *Camillus, or Rome Delivered*. This tragedy was enacted with great success in the Bunins' private theater by the author himself and his young friends.

Zhukovsky began his schooling at Tula in the private pensionat of Khristofor Rodé and later continued in the Tula public school; however, his powers of concentration were poor, and the strictly compulsory nature of the lessons was repellent to him. The future poet was subsequently expelled from the school "for lack of ability" but proceeded to make much more satisfactory progress at home with the aid of tutors hired for him and his young female relatives.

In 1797 the boy was removed from Tula and placed in a pensionat for the nobility attached to the University of Moscow. The headmaster of the pensionat, A. A. Prokopovich-Antonsky, was a writer and pedagogue having Masonic connections with groups that had been broken up by Catherine II, who greatly disapproved of them. However, the director of the University of Moscow, I. P. Turgenev, was also a Freemason who saw to it that his students were educated in concepts of moral self-improvement, philanthropy, civic duty, and—at the same time—political loyalty.

Zhukovsky was profoundly affected by these ideals of self-development and individual virtue, which he interpreted as being not only personal, but also social; he remained essentially faithful to them throughout his life. The friends of his youth, however, Andrey and Nikolay Turgenev, who, as students, had been brought up in the same traditions, followed very different paths: one, to become a liberal freethinker; the other, a revolutionary.

In 1798, Zhukovsky delivered an oration in his pensionat "On Virtue," and in the same year gave a recitation of a poem—one of the earliest to have been preserved—also entitled "Virtue" ("Dobrodetel' "). It was quite obvious that the theme he had chosen was for him no mere obligatory moralistic exercise.

Gradually, literary work came to dominate the young author's interests and even assumed a certain practical significance for him. Since he lacked the money to acquire all the books that interested him, Zhukovsky translated several popular sentimental works by the German dramatist August Kotzebue, and earned seventy-five rubles for the translation of one of his novels, *Die jüngsten Kinder meiner Laune*, which Zhukovsky reentitled *The Boy by the Stream* (*Mal'chik u ruch'ia*).

By the standards of the day, the pensionat offered a good education; among its teachers were professors from the University of Moscow. In the literary division, in which Zhukovsky was pursuing his studies, humanistic interests predominated, and literary pursuits were extensively encouraged. The best essays by pupils were recommended to such Moscow journals as *Agreeable and Useful Pastime (Priyatnoe i poleznoe preprovozhdenie vremeni)*, *Dawn (Utrenniaia zaria)*, and others. Another good point was that the other youths studying at the pensionat were also bright students and provided a sympathetic milieu for the young poet.

Some friendships formed at the pensionat were to endure throughout Zhukovsky's lifetime. His relationship with the sons of I. P. Turgenev, who, in his turn, had been on good terms with Zhukovsky's father, has passed into the history of Russian culture as a model of deep, idealistic, and romantic friendship. Zhukovsky was especially close to the third son, Andrey, his elder by two years, at that time already a student at the university. Together with the promising writer Andrey Kaysarov, Andrey Turgenev organized a group of educated young people to which Zhukovsky owed much. Virtue, poetry, friendship, nature, and pure love were proclaimed by these young men as the foundation of human happiness. The literary tastes of the group tended toward the sentimental, and it was here that Zhukovsky first discovered the German Preromantic literature of *Sturm und Drang*, in particular, Goethe and Schiller.

Melancholy, frequently purely abstract sadness, and sorrowful forebodings, much of which was the reflection of contemporary literary taste, became unexpectedly associated with real tragedy; in 1803 Andrey Turgenev caught a chill and died. The image of his friend always remained fresh in Zhukovsky's memory, and he felt this death to be a fateful confirmation of the mutability of all worldly things.

The poet had become profoundly imbued with the concepts of eternal love and of friendship beyond the grave, with the idea that only on "the heavenly shore" did earthly beauty attain true, full life. Many years later, in connection with other, similar experiences, the poet was to write: "There in *heavenly* incorruption/You will gain all *earthly* good . . ." ("The Traveler").[2]

The emotional side of Zhukovsky's life was predetermined at an early stage by his readiness to accept moral sacrifice, suffering, and the inevitability of worldly loss. This readiness set the tone of his friendships and, later, of his love.

II *First Steps in Literature: The Influence of Karamzin*

Zhukovsky's literary debut was made at the very beginning of his school days at the pensionat. The poet was only fourteen when his article "Thoughts Before a Tomb" ("Mysli pri grobnitse") was published in the journal *Agreeable and Useful Pastime*. After this came the poems "May Morning" ("Maiskoe utro"), "Virtue," the articles "Peace and War" ("Mir i voina"), "The True Hero" ("Istinnyi geroi"), and others. By the time he left the pensionat, Zhukovsky had published nearly fifteen works. This fact did not by any means signify that the young man had at all succeeded in making his name. In his day literature was confined to a very small circle; writers were counted by tens, not hundreds of thousands, whereas there were a comparatively large number of journals.

When he finished school, Zhukovsky entered the civil service in the Moscow office of the salt industry, a position he left after a few months. His friend and biographer, Karl Zeydlits, tells us that in later life the poet made a joke of this first, most ill-chosen position. It was clear both to the future poet himself and to his friends that any form of office work could only hinder and distort the development of his maturing talent. Zhukovsky then left for home, returning to "Mishenskoe" and taking with him a not inconsiderable library.

By 1802, Zhukovsky was fully aware of his literary vocation. The first serious test he set for himself was a free translation of the "Elegy Written in a Country Churchyard" by the English sentimentalist poet Thomas Gray. He undertook this task for the best Russian literary journal, Karamzin's *Messenger of Europe* (*Vestnik Evropy*).

The young poet's earlier literary experiments paled before this masterpiece. Zhukovsky himself always spoke of the year 1802 as the first in his literary life and of the translation of Gray's "Elegy" as his first published work.

Zhukovsky's "Country Churchyard" was immediately acclaimed as a model of elegiac form; it was quoted in one breath with verses by the best Russian poets of the day. Nikolay Karamzin, the leader of the Russian sentimentalist school in literature, drew the young author into his own circle and foretold a brilliant future for him. They remained friends for many years, and it was Karamzin who later recommended Zhukovsky to the Imperial family, a recommendation which played a most important part in the poet's life.

Karamzin had a decisive influence upon the development of Zhukovsky's opinions and poetical style. The older author's work reflected the mentality induced by the reaction of European intellectuals to the great and tragic events of the end of the eighteenth century—to the French Revolution and its immediate consequences. He was convinced that, on principle, the use of force could never lead to real improvement in the destiny of man. In his attitude toward the past, as in his evaluation of the present, Karamzin was an advocate of philanthropy, the golden mean, and moderation in all things. Peaceful evolution for society and moral self-improvement for the individual were, in his view, the natural means at the disposal of mankind. By and large, Zhukovsky accepted and shared Karamzin's sociopolitical views.

In Karamzin's works, social issues are always subordinated to the moral. According to Karamzin, every man, whoever he may be, merits respect and sympathy if he is "virtuous" and prompted by honorable thoughts and impulses. This tenet is the cornerstone of Karamzin's sentimentalism, which is concerned above all with the depiction of feelings and emotions. One of the favorite subjects of the Sentimentalist school was the love of a nobleman for a poor peasant girl, a love that softened and blurred the harsh outlines of social inequality. An example is the story *Poor Liza (Bednaya Liza)*, the literary archetype for this subject. Karamzin himself, however, unlike some of his less-gifted imitators, was not prone to naive optimism; he gave his famous story a tragic ending.

During the first two decades of the nineteenth century, before writers from among the revolutionary nobility appeared on the scene, namely, the Decembrists and young Pushkin, Karamzin's influence dominated literary life. Belinsky was fully justified in commenting that the entire period, from Karamzin to Pushkin, should bear the name of Karamzin.[3]

The central figure of Gray's "Elegy" (which had been translated into Russian—far less successfully—before Zhukovsky) is the image of the poet-dreamer, deeply sensitive to the dissonances and injustices of life, full of sympathy for the "little", obscure laborers whose "humble annals" are hidden beneath the stones of the village graveyard. Fate has been unjust to these people, yet, on the other hand, since power and glory, in the opinion of the poet, are inextricably entwined with the temptations and vices of society, whereas the highest good is to maintain the moral dignity of man, the elegy is in essence a glorification of the modest lot of the simple villager.

Stylistically, the "Village Churchyard" was also in full accord with "Karamzinian" principles. While working on his translation, Zhukovsky modeled himself on Karamzin's lyric poetry (on such pieces, for example, as the elegy "On Melancholy"), but he perfected the style to a remarkable degree. Simplicity of language, sincerity of inspiration, emotion, and lyricism—all these characteristics placed Zhukovsky's "Village Churchyard" at the very center of the nascent new poetry.

The elegy, the song (romance), and the friendly epistle are the basic genres of Zhukovsky's early period. The elegy attracted him by its subject matter, which had already been determined by European tradition: thoughts on the vanity of earthly life, absorption in the poet's own, inner world, a dreamy sensitivity to nature.

The second masterpiece of Zhukovsky's early lyric poetry was the elegy "Evening" ("Vecher," 1806), marked by the same qualities as the "Village Churchyard," "Evening" is a meditative elegy. Here, the poet's thoughts, or meditations, are focused on a personal theme. Reminiscences of lost friends and passing youth are mingled with a dreamy, melancholic response to the evening landscape. In this elegy, Zhukovsky's language is at once poetic and unconstrained.

After the year 1802, which saw Zhukovsky make his name in literature, Karamzin opened his house to the young poet, welcoming him whenever he cared to come to stay, so that he now divided his time between the Bunin country estate and Karamzin's home near Moscow. Apparently under the influence of the historical interests of his older friend and patron, Zhukovsky wrote the story of "Vadim of Novgorod" ("Vadim Novgorodskii"), a parallel to Karamzin's tale of "Marfa Posadnitsa," in which subtle psychological motivation is ascribed to the actions of historical personages.

Zhukovsky had developed as a pro-European but one whose wide knowledge of, and admiration for, the cultural heritage of the enlightened peoples of Europe in no way prevented him from being an ardent patriot.

All through the first decade of the nineteenth century, a fateful conflict had been brewing with Napoleon's France. In 1806, the author of the tenderly elegiac "Village Churchyard" and "Evening" wrote a solemn ode, "The Lay of the Bard upon the Grave of the Victorious Slavs," in which he reminded Russian society of the glories of its past. This poem also was accorded a very favorable reception, and was republished several times.

At about this time Karamzin, completely absorbed in his labors as a historian, gave up not only his lighter writing, but also his publishing activities. The journal he had made famous, *The Messenger of Europe*, passed from one hand to another and began to deteriorate. Zhukovsky was offered the editorship. This was a token of great respect and confidence in the young poet, who had already begun to play a decisive role in literature, although in his private life he enjoyed no social standing at all and was living as resident tutor in the household of his sister, Ekaterina Afanasevna Protasova. The poet accepted the job and moved to Moscow, where he set about energetically reviving *The Messenger of Europe*. Over a brief period in 1808–09, he wrote several articles in which he laid down the journal's policy. They included: "On the Obligations of a Journalist"; "The Writer and Society"; "On the Moral Usefulness of Poetry" (a translation of an article by Johann Engel); and "On the Fable and Krylov's Fables." These writings propagated the notion that art was a most effective means of moral education. In two of the articles he wrote for the *Messenger of Europe*, he touched on the question of serfdom in Russia.

Zhukovsky's reputation as a leading poet was confirmed by the publication of the ballad "Lyudmila" in *The Messenger of Europe* (1808).

In European literature of the second half of the eighteenth century and the first half of the nineteenth century, the ballad, with its origins in poetic folk tradition, was extremely popular. The ballad was distinguished by a taste for "wonders" and "horrors"— everything that could not be strictly accounted for by reason—the emotional element predominating over the rational, intensity of feeling over analysis. The vogue for this genre was characteristic of the Romantic movement in poetry.

The ballad became one of Zhukovsky's favorite genres. His models were the ballads of Bürger, Uhland, Scott, Schiller, Goethe, and, in Russian literature, Karamzin's "Raisa." It was in his ballads that Zhukovsky's Romantic leanings found their most vivid expression.

Zhukovsky's "Lyudmila" was a free adaptation of Bürger's "Lenore". Eager both to make his characters as comprehensible to his readers as possible and at the same time to solve one of the problems confronting the Russian literature of his day by creating a form for the Russian ballad, Zhukovsky transformed Uhland's figures from medieval Germans into Russian youths and maidens, set the scene in sixteenth century Russia, and introduced the national and patriotic motif of the Livonian wars (1558–1583). Zhukovsky achieved still greater renown with the ballad "Svetlana" (1808–1812). Its subject was also based on Bürger's "Lenore."

III *Love for Masha Protasova.*
Participation in the War of 1812.
The Blossoming of Lyric Poetry.

The peculiar circumstances of Zhukovsky's birth were to have a fateful effect on his emotional life. The poet lived for several years as resident tutor in the family of his sister, Ekaterina Afanasevna Protasova, instructing her daughters Mariya (Masha) and Aleksandra. The poet put much thought and imagination into the education of the two girls, which he directed for about three years. It was, in fact, this experience in teaching general history and the history of the arts to two young girls of whom he was extremely fond that gave Zhukovsky his taste for pedagogy.

Although Zhukovsky and Ekaterina Protasova had the same father, he did not consider himself her brother. He had known her daughters, his nieces, since they were quite small. As they grew up, he fell in love with the elder, Masha, and this love set his feet upon a thorny path. The only happiness granted the poet was the knowledge that he was deeply loved in return. Zhukovsky's love for Masha permeated all his poetry and had a decisive influence on the course of his life.

Neither Masha nor Zhukovsky desired an "illicit" love. Knowing the circumstances of the poet's own birth, we should not be surprised that he took no decisive step, when Ekaterina Protasova refused her consent to their marriage on religious grounds, to make Masha his wife in fact, if not in name. The poet was acutely aware that there could be no happiness for them outside of a strictly legal union. Zhukovsky's gentle, considerate nature was of course also a contributing factor in his decision.

The poet's friends followed the course of his unhappy romance, which lasted for many years, with sympathy and anxiety. Aleksandr Turgenev sought to interest individual churchmen whose approval might have been accepted by Masha's mother. These authorities, however, would not express a categorical opinion. Thus, the poet's entire youth passed in a hopeless struggle for personal happiness.

The numerous Bunin clan were, on the whole, sympathetic to the lovers, even offered to plead their cause before the mother, but, when it came to the sticking point, failed. Zhukovsky had ample opportunity to convince himself that his hopes were ill-founded, but he still kept hoping. He was not in the least passive, he did not yield, indeed he persisted, thinking up one plan after another to effect their union. Perseverence was the magic password for him and Masha.

In the years 1808 and 1809, Zhukovsky put his feelings for Masha into the love story "Maria's Grove" ("Mar'ina roshcha"). On the first page, in Uslad's monologue, we find an echo of Petrarch, in essence a prose translation of Sonnet CCCI from the book "On the Life of my Lady Laura."

Zhukovsky's sentiments for Masha Protasova also inspired his love poems. During the first period, from 1808 to 1812, Zhukovsky's poetry, both original and translated, was imbued with profoundly lyrical feeling. He adhered to the canons of the sentimental style but, unlike other poets of his day, succeeded in rising above its artificial conventions. His mind and character harmonized with the ideals of Sentimentalist literature.

Nevertheless, in his real-life relations, Zhukovsky by no means purposely cultivated a plight suggested by literature. In this attitude he differed from many Romantic poets, followers of Byron, Novalis, or—somewhat earlier—Goethe. Any kind of stylization, even the most "natural," was alien to him, and he did not think of his life as "a work of art." In this conviction lay Zhukovsky's affinity with Pre-romantic, rationalist culture.

Zhukovsky's poetry was always the expression of real life. For a long time, for example, he was forced to conceal his love, since he was far from certain of the possibility of a happy ending—as events proved, quite rightly so. It is the outpourings of his own heart that are expressed by personae of his love lyrics and verses, most of which are adaptations from the German. These poems include "Longing for the Beloved" ("Toska po milom") from the song by Schiller; "A Song" ("Pesnia"); and "My Friend, My Guardian-Angel" ("Moy drug, khranitel'-angel moy") from the French of Philippe Fabré d'Eglantine; "To Her" ("K nei"), a free translation of an anonymous German song; "A Song" ("Pesnia"), and "O, Dearest Friend! Now Thou Art Joyful" ("O milyi drug! teper' s toboiu radost' ") by Christophe August Tiedge. It is quite possible that not only the nature of Zhukovsky's gift but also his own situation drove him to seek "models" in his translations which he could make speak as it were in his own name, yet *not* in his own name. This theory also explains to some extent the lack of details from real life in his lyrics, the sentimental, literary quality of the lyrical subjects, the characteristic "he" and "she."

The year 1812 found Zhukovsky at a crossroads in his career. A year before, both his "mothers"—Elizaveta Dementevna and Mariya Grigorevna Bunina—had died at almost the same time. The poet's youth was behind him. He knew himself, knew that his nature was essentially contemplative and that what he required was not "tempests," but peace of mind. When the War of 1812 broke out the poet was perfectly aware from the beginning that he was not made for military service, and thus avoided the disillusionment that might have ensued. Like all those with whom he came in contact, he was, however, caught up in the sweeping tide of patriotic enthusiasm, and when in July a manifesto was published on the formation of military forces to combat the armies of Napoleon, Zhukovsky decided to enlist in the militia. At the same time, he asked for Masha Protasova's hand, convinced that the family should unite more closely than ever in the face of the trials that lay ahead. He met with a firm refusal from the mother of his beloved and left Muratovo for Moscow with a heavy heart. In August Zhukovsky was accepted for the Moscow militia with the rank of lieutenant. On the day of the Battle of Borodino—August 26, 1812 (old style)—he was in the reserve, to the rear of the main army, and was subsequently recommended to Field Marshal Kutuzov for duty with the staff of the Commander-in-Chief.

For Zhukovsky the War of 1812 set in motion a wave of patriotic feeling. His attitude toward the war typified the mood of all progressive circles in Russian society. However, he was not required to take any very active part in the fighting, since in the early stages the militia was held in reserve and the poet heard only the echoes of battles. In the autumn of 1812, Zhukovsky fell ill and was incapacitated for some time. In 1813, he retired from military service. "I . . . followed the colors not for rank or medals . . . but because at *such a time* it is every man's *duty* to be a soldier, even if he has no inclination."[4]

A memorial to Zhukovsky's patriotic enthusiasm and one of the most vivid poetic works of the War of 1812 was his poem "A Bard in the Camp of the Russian Warriors" ("Pevets vo stane russkikh voinov"). The "Bard" paved the way for a new treatment of the patriotic theme, devoid of rhetoric and "odic pathos":

> Our native land, my friends, I toast!
>   That sky beneath whose dome
> Life's sweetness was to us disclosed:
>   The fields, the hills of home,
> That land beside whose homely streams
>   We wandered first as boys,
> Where first we dreamt youth's golden dreams,
>   Learnt lessons, played with toys.
> Ah, what can with your charm compete?
>   O sacred land of birth,
> What heart can fail to miss a beat
>   When blessing native earth?

(I, 151)

A particularly important theme of the "Bard" is that of friendship. As a traditional theme of Sentimental poetry, its role in this poem is to color the whole with an intimate lyric quality. At the same time, its function is not only intimate but also civic, for it serves to symbolize the unity of the Russian soldiers. The very concept of building up a patriotic feeling capable of appealing to many generations of the Russian people was one that created an impression of indissoluble solidarity, continuity, and unity. The many heroes whose praises the "bard" sings in this poem appear less as "leaders" than as representatives of this unity: their very numbers indicate how general and widespread was the patriotic enthusiasm of the day.

From 1812 to 1817, until the beginning of extensive activity on the part of the oppositional secret societies in Russia, Zhukovsky was regarded as a poet of civic sentiment and thoughts. The patriotic ideas of Russian society, still associated with the struggle against Napoleon, had not yet been transformed into ideas of political freethinking. This would come after 1818, when the government embarked upon a repressive policy. The popular program of the moment was one of enlightened monarchy, of liberalization "from above." The voice of "The Bard in the Camp of the Russian Warriors" was accepted by society as the voice of Russia itself. This was precisely what Pushkin had in mind when he wrote in one of his letters to Zhukovsky: "No one had more right than you to say: 'the voice of the lyre is the voice of the people.' "[5]

In 1815, Zhukovsky was offered an appointment as reader to Her Imperial Majesty, Mariya Fyodorovna. He did not immediately realize what radical changes in his life this appointment would bring. At the time, he was completely engrossed in his own personal life, in which new complications had arisen. Masha and her mother had gone to live in the city of Dorpat (Tartu), following Aleksandra, whose husband had been offered a chair at the university there. The poet spent much time in Dorpat, where he made the acquaintance of German scholars and German philosophy as well as that of his future biographer, the young student Karl Zeydlits. In literary and scholarly circles in Dorpat, Zhukovsky was received with the greatest respect as one of the luminaries of the Russian literature of the day; he attended official gatherings at the university, where he was treated as an honored guest. In the meantime, the situation in Aleksandra's family had gone from bad to worse, because of her husband's hysterical and unprincipled character.

In 1817, Masha made the decision to obtain the right at least to an open "fraternal friendship" with Zhukovsky by becoming the wife of another man. She married a professor of medicine, Johann Moyer, bore him a daughter, and died in her second childbirth in 1823.

During the five years following the crisis year of 1817, much changed in Zhukovsky's life. He himself changed. "The moment at which I made up my mind made me a different person," he wrote of his consent to Masha's marriage. "I took a draft of the waters of Lethe and found them conducive to sleep. My soul softened! Happily, there were no stains left upon it; on the other hand, it is as white as paper on which nothing has been written. This nothing is my present sickness, just as dangerous as the first, and almost like death."[6]

Masha was attached to her husband but wrote in her diary that in moments of sadness only one word had the power to soothe her, and then only when uttered aloud: "Zhukovsky!" For Moyer, a man of remarkable nobility of character, Zhukovsky preserved a lifelong friendship. Moyer died twenty years after his wife, with her name on his lips.

From 1815 on, the influence of German writers upon Zhukovsky's poetry became more marked. The original impulse derived from his frequent visits to Dorpat; later, it was closely associated with his duties at the court. He was deeply impressed by Novalis of the Jena Romantics. He met Ludwig Tieck, and through Schiller's theoretical works he came to accept much of Kant's philosophy.

The dreamy, imaginative quality typical of so many of his early works grew organically into a mystic conception of two worlds—the hidden world of essence and the visible world of appearances. Zhukovsky's mysticism, markedly religious in character, was nourished primarily by his Christian faith in the immortality of the soul. This conviction provided the basis for the poet's acceptance of the more extreme forms of Romantic mysticism. His simple, childlike faith had always admitted the hope that, in the world beyond the grave, he would find loved ones who had passed on before, exactly as they had been on earth.

> Farewell! Life cannot last! We'll meet yet, you and I,
> A rendezvous beyond the grave's our destination!
> Ah, happy certainty! Delightful expectation!
> With what a merry heart I'll meet my turn to die!
> (On the Death of Andrey Turgenev, 1803 [I, 35])

The longer he lived, the more steadfastly and passionately did Zhukovsky concentrate on the concept of the ephemeral nature of earthly happiness and the enduring quality of heavenly blessings.

IV   Career at Court. German Literary Influences. Hostile Criticism. Relations with Pushkin.

In the fateful year of 1817, when the poet "lost everything," a new sphere of activity opened up before him which was to absorb his energies increasingly and fill the vacuum within him. He was asked to become teacher of Russian to Princess Charlotte, Aleksandra Fyodorovna, the wife of the Grand Prince Nikolay Pavlovich, the future Nicholas I. The appointment was not such a sinecure as the previous one as reader to the Empress Mariya Fyodorovna. Aleksandra Fyodorovna later provided a very frank and succinct assessment of Zhukovsky's efforts: "As my teacher, I was given Vasily Andreevich Zhukovsky, a poet already famous; he was too much the poet to be a good teacher. Instead of keeping to the study of grammar, a single word would inspire him with an idea, the idea demanded to be expressed in a poem, the poem became a subject for discussion, and in this way almost all our lessons were spent; that is why I have such a poor command of the Russian language."[7] As time passed, Zhukovsky became more and more accustomed to his new circle, and particularly to its female constituent. Official,

"male" court life, that is, the political aspects of life at court, remained, for the time being, a closed book to him. In this course of
events, one cannot fail to perceive the outlines of the family "model"
which had accustomed the poet to predominantly female society
from his earliest years.

His journeys to Dorpat left a bitter taste, so the poet sought relief
in his new career. He accompanied his "pupil," Aleksandra
Fyodorovna, on her visits to her native Germany, where he even
became friendly with the Crown Prince and Aleksandra
Fyodorovna's brother, Friedrich Wilhelm III, the future king of
Prussia. There is no reason to suppose that these developments
turned the poet's head. Nevertheless, he did take part constantly in
court amusements, expressing admiration for his "pupil" in amateur
court theatricals and *tableaux vivants*. In one of these she represented an Indian princess, the heroine of Thomas Moore's *Lalla
Rookh*, thereby inspiring one of the poet's most romantic poems.

At court Zhukovsky became more and more engrossed in his
duties; on the whole, this preoccupation exerted an adverse effect
upon his poetic development. In the first place, he was gradually
transferring his energies, normally devoted to creative work, to
teaching. Another factor was the increase in his poetic production of
motifs derived from German Romantic mysticism. This increase was
not the direct result of his contact with the cultural milieu of
"Princess Charlotte," as Aleksandra Fyodorovna had been addressed
in her own country. The development of a poet of Zhukovsky's
stature could have been guided only by his own inner creative
impulses. Although several original and translated works of the
period 1818 to 1823 were written at the request of his "royal pupil,"
Zhukovsky's orientation toward German Romantic idealism pre-
dated his appointment to the German princess. It was only in the
natural course of the creative process that this orientation should
have led to the absorption of its influence at a deeper level of consciousness.

In 1818, a limited edition of Zhukovsky's adaptations and original
verses in German and Russian was published under the title *Für
wenige (For the Few)*. The title of this collection earned Zhukovsky
many reproaches, both from his contemporaries and from later
generations. The collection consisted essentially of works from
German poetry translated by the poet into Russian with "pedagogic"
intent and was meant perhaps primarily, but not, of course, exclu-

sively for use in court circles. It was widely read. The title was not
designed to convey that obviously "courtly" meaning it might well
be understood, if mistakenly, to imply: it stems, in fact, from
Horace's aphorism: "Do not wish to astound the crowd but write for
the few." The young Pushkin placed the correct interpretation upon
the formula "for the few" when he addressed Zhukovsky with the
following verses:

> Your poems are for *the few* indeed,
> Not written for the envious crews
> Of critics, or the paltry breed
> That feed on others' news and views,
> But for stern friends of genius,
> For friends of sacred verity . . .
> . . . Who in the fine to find delight
> A fine vocation have received
> And through your rapture have perceived
> Their rapture as a burning light.
>
> (Pushkin, II, 59)

Some of Zhukovsky's works on the fates and personages of the
Royal Family are very profound, as, for example, "On the Death of
Her Majesty the Queen of Württemberg" and "The Flower of the
Covenant." The latter was written on a theme suggested by
Aleksandra Fyodorovna herself.

Yet there was something about the poet's "courtly romanticism"
which could not fail to irritate many of his contemporaries. Within
the pale of the court circle the poet made himself too secure from
the future and saw the historical element of political life in terms of
the court. To be sure, he was not indifferent to politics, as it would
sometimes seem. He was a convinced monarchist; he could not
conceive of any other form of government for Russia and never tired
of repeating that the people's fate depended upon the degree of
cultivation of the mind and spirit of the reigning monarch. Hence
derived his belief that "the history of the royal soul"[8] was immensely
important in the history of Russia; the poet became increasingly
absorbed by the prospect of educating and perfecting this soul. In
essence, Zhukovsky pinned his hopes to a belief in a political
"miracle," the possibility of changing the whole history of Russian
czarism by means of an inner spiritual transformation.

He did not share the political enthusiasms of the revolutionary youth of the nobility during the first half of the 1820s, years so pregnant with stormy events. He behaved as though they did not exist. This was the weakness of his position. He caused extreme vexation among the Decembrists—the future participants in the December, 1825 uprising against czarism. In 1819, Zhukovsky rejected a proposal by the Decembrist Sergey Petrovich Trubetskoy that he should join a secret society (we should not forget, however, that throughout the ensuing years he never betrayed the secret which was entrusted to him at that time, the fact of such a society's existence in Russia).

The Decembrist writers objected strongly to Zhukovsky's elegiac "melancholy," which carried within itself the seeds of extreme pessimism. But they were impressed by the ode, a genre to which civic themes and pathos lend themselves naturally. The Russian ode of the end of the eighteenth century was founded on an optimistic philosophy of enlightenment.

In the first half of the 1820s, the Decembrists and their sympathizers also condemned Zhukovsky for the dominance of translations in his work, for his lack of "fantasy," of original lyric and epic subjects. Even Pushkin criticized Zhukovsky on this score. Now, however, at a distance of a century and a half, we should surely reexamine this question. The Europeanism of Russian culture necessarily implied not only that Russian problems should be introduced to the general European arena but also that European problems should be included in the "orbit" of Russian consciousness. During that period it was certainly not only Zhukovsky who devoted a large part of his energies to translations and adaptations. His antagonist Pavel Katenin was, and is, known primarily as the translator of Racine's *Andromaque* and other works of the French Classical school. Many of Batyushkov's best works are adaptations and free translations. Kondraty Ryleev's "Thoughts" ("Dumy") were suggested to him by the historical "songs" of the Polish poet Julian Niemcewicz. Pushkin, as we know, often deliberately chose subjects already familiar in world literature. And, although Pushkin's genius was distinguished by quite exceptional originality, in the 1830s even he was accused of imitating Byron (for *Evgeny Onegin*), Shakespeare (for *Boris Godunov*), and Walter Scott (for "The Captain's Daughter").

On this level of criticism we should distinguish in Zhukovsky's work, too, between lyrics and ballads, on the one hand, and epic and drama, on the other. These sources provided material for his original work, helped to construct his own poetic world, and were endowed with a vividly expressed individual style. In the epic and drama, Zhukovsky did indeed set himself tasks as a translator. Zhukovsky was a lyrical poet *par excellence*, but at the same time he deserves great recognition for having enriched Russian poetry with epic and dramatic translations of the highest quality.

The creative and personal relationship between Pushkin and Zhukovsky constitutes an important page in the history of Russian literature. All his life Pushkin held Zhukovsky in profound respect and affection; he often confided to him matters he preferred not to disclose to others.

As distinct from the complex relationship between Pushkin and Karamzin, Pushkin's attitude toward Zhukovsky underwent no changes. It was Zhukovsky to whom he had wished to dedicate *Boris Godunov*; only Karamzin's death and a request from his daughter altered that decision. Zhukovsky's attitude toward Pushkin was one of quite exceptional solicitude and attention; he recognized him as a great poet, the pride of Russia; he did everything in his power to protect him, at first from governmental persecution, and later—in the 1830s—from being baited by the "society mob." Unfortunately, during the final period of Pushkin's life, Zhukovsky failed to understand that Pushkin's only possible salvation would have been severance of all relations with the court. Instead, he did all he could to dissuade Pushkin from retiring from his position at court; in this attitude, of course, Zhukovsky's own illusions about the court came to the fore. Under the circumstances, however, it is difficult to blame Zhukovsky; he, too, was mistaken, just as Pushkin's closest friends were mistaken about him in that last period of his life.

Zhukovsky saw Pushkin's death in January of 1837 as an irreparable national tragedy. It was only after the passing of his great colleague that Zhukovsky was informed of all the details of the treacherous intrigue that had been woven about Pushkin and also learned how the police had made his life a burden with their ceaseless surveillance.

Zhukovsky expressed his profound indignation at all this in a letter to the head of the political police, Aleksandr Khristoforovich Benkendorf, written in February or March of 1837. We do not know to this day incidentally whether Benkendorf ever actually read the letter. Meanwhile, in order to ensure the preservation and publication of the works of the great poet, Zhukovsky, in all his letters and reviews, emphasized Pushkin's political loyalty. This aim is noticeable even in his remarkable letter to the poet's father, Sergey Lvovich Pushkin, written on February 15, 1837. This long letter contains a most valuable account of Pushkin's last moments and is composed with great love and bitter grief. These are the same two sentiments that pervade his poem: "He Lay Without Movement . . . " ("On lezhal bez dvizheniia . . .").

The personal friendship between Pushkin and Zhukovsky was based primarily on their respect for each other's work. As early as 1815, when he first heard the young Pushkin's poem "Memories of Tsarskoe Selo" ("Vospominaniia o Tsarskom sele") Zhukovsky had exclaimed: "Here is a real poet come among us!" For Pushkin, Zhukovsky was his "confidant, guardian, and keeper" (*Ruslan and Lyudmila*). In 1830, in the rough drafts for the eighth chapter of *Evgeny Onegin*, Pushkin speaks of Zhukovsky with enthusiasm and gratitude as a poet of the first rank, hailing his first creative steps in one breath with those of Derzhavin:

> You, brimming with deep inspiration,
> Singer of all that's beautiful . . .[9]

Particularly well known are Pushkin's lines on the elder poet occurring in his poem "To the Portrait of Zhukovsky" ("K portretu Zhukovskogo"): "And the beguiling sweetness of his verses will long outlast the length of envious years . . . ." In Pushkin's correspondence there are some extremely interesting pages of polemics against the Decembrists in defense of Zhukovsky. In contradistinction to the Decembrists, Pushkin considered Zhukovsky's influence on contemporary letters, on "the spirit of our literature," to be beneficent, and more significant that Batyushkov's.

In Pushkin's work one does find friendly parodies of Zhukovsky. But malicious parodies of Zhukovsky as poet evoked Pushkin's indignation, and he dismissed them as signs of archaic, or plain bad, taste. Pushkin perceived in Zhukovsky a poet of stature, a serious poet, the only contemporary poet whom he could consider an equal.

Like many of his contemporaries, Zhukovsky held that the development of the epic form was essential to Russian poetry. As far back as 1814 he had planned to write an original, legendary heroic poem, *Vladimir*, on a subject taken from the history of ancient

Russia. However, he never accomplished the task he had set himself; he postponed its execution and subsequent events diverted his attention. After Pushkin wrote *Ruslan and Lyudmila*, Zhukovsky felt the problem of the epic had been brilliantly resolved. He presented Pushkin with his own likeness, on which he inscribed the famous words: "To the victorious pupil from his vanquished teacher." Toward 1820, Zhukovsky translated into modern Russian the *Lay of the Host of Igor*, a narrative poem preserved from Russia's distant, Kievan past; he revealed a remarkable sensitivity for the contemporary reader's expectations of the poem.

The appearance of Zhukovsky's translation of Schiller's tragedy *The Maid of Orleans* was a milestone in Russian literary history. It revitalized Russian drama of the 1820s, both by its patriotic and psychological content and by the novelty of its form. Schiller had been one of the first to approach the heroic theme from the point of view of its psychological impact. The structure of *The Maid of Orleans*, at variance with the accepted canons of classical drama in almost all respects, and especially so in its verse form—blank iambic pentameters—undoubtedly exercised a certain influence on Pushkin's *Boris Godunov*. Zhukovsky was attracted by the combination of religious and patriotic fervor in *The Maid of Orleans*.

In 1824, Zhukovsky's *Collected Works*, the crowning achievement of his "lyrical" period, were published. After this event, he would return to lyric poetry only occasionally.

The exhaustion of Zhukovsky's lyric inspiration was unquestionably linked with his career at court, a fact his friends, including Pushkin, resented. Apropos the publication of the *Collected Works*, Pushkin even wrote: "The late-lamented was a good man, may he rest in peace."[10] It was not only Zhukovsky's court career, however, that was responsible for the waning of his inspiration. It was as if Zhukovsky were yielding his place to Pushkin, of whose superiority he was fully aware. Not being envious by nature, Zhukovsky had felt no bitterness, only a sense of satisfaction, knowing himself to be the teacher and forerunner of Pushkin.

During the decade of the 1820s, Zhukovsky's poetry influenced the entire "Pushkin Pleiad," as well as such important poets as Baratynsky, Tyutchev, and the young Mikhail Lermontov.

From 1825 on, the attitude of the Decembrist writers toward Zhukovsky began to change. After the fiasco of December, 1825, on the Senate Square in St. Petersburg, their own writings became more and more tragic in nature. Ryleev, one of five condemned to death then, perished on the gallows in July of 1826. Those of the Decembrists who remained alive had been subjected to an immense ideological and psychological shock, and they read Zhukovsky with new eyes. In their own lyric poetry, the years of forced labor and exile produced an increase in elegiac motifs and introspective moods.

V *Zhukovsky After the Decembrist Rising*

At the beginning of a new period in Russian history, in the year 1826, when Nicholas I began his long reign against a background of portentous and threatening events, Zhukovsky was invited to organize and supervise the education of the heir to the throne, the future Alexander II.

The poet accepted the appointment, regarding it as his sacred mission as a citizen. Now, however, it became very difficult to find peaceful moments in which to concentrate on his poetry; sometimes whole years would pass without his producing any original work. The methodical elaboration and teaching of almost all subjects, except the purely military disciplines, took up all his time.

Zhukovsky undoubtedly did have an influence on the heir to the throne; he did his best to imbue him with his own views and was liked and trusted by his pupil to an extent that Nicholas I frequently found annoying.

In this context, the following letter written by Zhukovsky to the heir to the throne after he had come of age and Zhukovsky's task as mentor had ended, is not without interest. "My state business with you is over. . . . Now my loyalty to you consists in this: that I should, without respect of persons, pass on to you all thoughts and feelings which seem to me to be true. I know that your heart is akin to mine, that mine will always find a response in yours. And it is in this pure commerce of love and truth that my connection with the heir to the throne will consist from now onward. . . . The limits which separate you from others cannot and should not be my limits: I am closer to you, not by rank, but by virtue of our past which has placed you under obligations to me which you cannot in the nature of things be under to anyone else, and from which high office does not absolve you. . . . This will be no infringement of the uninfringeable rights of your office, it will be the high dignity of man, and it is man, in whatever rank of office, that is most important."[11]

The poet sought to use his position to obtain an improvement in the lot of the exiled Decembrist revolutionaries; with remarkable persistence he never ceased in his efforts on their behalf, although they invariably brought down upon him the wrath of the tsar.

It was at Zhukovsky's plea that Aleksandr Herzen was transferred to Vladimir from exile in Vyatka; afterward, Nicholas I was wont to say grimly that he "would never forget" Zhukovsky's part in this event.

Among those foreign diplomats who were seeking to gain a clearer picture of the situation at court, Zhukovsky was considered almost the head of the liberal party. This was not, of course, the case, but his reputation did in fact reflect the impression of independence and firmness of principle that Zhukovsky produced upon all who met him.

In the years 1837 to 1839, Zhukovsky accompanied the heir to the throne on a journey through Russia and western Europe. During his stay in Siberia he stubbornly returned once again to the question of the fate of the Decembrists. Zhukovsky also expended much energy in his struggle for the emancipation from serfdom of the Ukrainian poet Taras Shevchenko. Zhukovsky's portrait, painted at his own expense by the fashionable artist Karl Bryullov, was put up as a prize for a lottery; the 2,500 rubles collected in this way were used to buy Shevchenko from his owner. Zhukovsky also took steps to obtain the emancipation of another serf writer, Aleksandr Vasilevich Nikitenko and his family.

The 1830s were, perhaps, the most contented years of the poet's life. The bitterness of his personal losses was no longer painfully acute. He enjoyed immense authority in society. Zhukovsky impressed everyone: the "Pushkin Pleiad"; Lermontov; the exiled Decembrists; the future revolutionary democrats Belinsky and Herzen; and many others.

During these years, the poet led a comparatively retired life; he was absorbed in his work, and, aside from this, he was no lover of fashionable diversions. The circle of friends he saw regularly included the family of Karamzin, who had died in 1826; Pyotr Vyazemsky, a friend of his youth; the poet Ivan Dmitriev; Aleksandr Pushkin; and Nikolay Gogol. In those years also, Zhukovsky engaged in the literary wars on the side of Pushkin and his circle. He had his own enemies, too: the undistinguished writer and omnipresent informer, Faddey Bulgarin, who persecuted Pushkin with his denunciations; and also various other people about the court, aristocrats who looked down on him because of his "low" birth.

Zhukovsky was hardly objective in his view of the Russian autocracy. He could not be because of his personal relations with the Royal Family which involved a genuine devotion to them shared by few of his fellow poets in the 1830s, and by still fewer in the 1840s. In this attitude Zhukovsky was swimming against the whole tide of the Russian society of his day, whose more thoughtful members had felt an emotional devotion to their tsar only for a short time, after the first victories over Napoleon.

The intentions of the Decembrist revolutionaries were profoundly alien to Zhukovsky, above all because of their terroristic aspect; the poet was horrified when, after the suppression of the conspiracy, he learned of their plans for the assassination of the Imperial Family.

Zhukovsky's convictions as regards the rightness and organic suitability of the tsarist regime in Russia were linked with his religious beliefs. The author of the tsarist national anthem ("God Save the Czar") looked upon the Russian monarch as the Lord's anointed. Zhukovsky had much in common with Gogol at the time the latter was writing his oft-maligned *Selected Passages from Correspondence with Friends* and, during the period 1845 to 1850, was himself the author of a number of articles on the autocracy of a religious and ethical nature.

Zhukovsky's political conservatism was a result of his whole ideological position. The key to his view of things was a religiosity that relegated social problems to second place. "God and the soul— these are the two realities. Everything else is a printed announcement pasted onto the minute," he wrote in his diary for the year 1821.

Zhukovsky conceived of the basis of social morality in terms of Christianity. In much that he wrote we may observe the sporadic flickering of thoughts later to be fully developed in Dostoevsky's novels (for example, the famous "all is permitted"). Zhukovsky wrote in his article "Enthusiasm and Enthusiasts," composed in the 1840s:

A brigand who slits the throat of a passer-by without any other motivation than to gain possession of his purse, deserves the gallows. But is the strongly motivated brigand any less deserving of such a reward, when, having stepped out onto the highway in the early morning, he puts to death a rich traveler in order to give away his gold to a pauper that same evening, a pauper whom he hopes to meet on that same road? But he may never meet that pauper; and night may overtake them both on the road before the sought-for meeting. . . . If there were to be one, *general* morality based on Christianity and equally applicable to everyone, then *private* morality will never be shaken.[12]

The conflict sketched here unconsciously reveals an affinity with Dostoevsky's *Crime and Punishment*.

The upheavals of 1848 in France frightened Zhukovsky, so that his conservatism assumed extreme forms. He dreamed that Russia might avoid Europe's political fate. "What is the aim of our present reformers? They do not perceive it with any clarity themselves. It is very probable that many of them are deceiving themselves, marching on ahead with banners on which are inscribed in glittering letters the catchwords of our century: *forward, liberty, development, humanity*—they themselves are convinced that their road leads directly to the promised land. And it may be that they, like so many of their predecessors, are destined to shudder at the brink or already in the depths of that abyss which will soon open up before them. . . ."[13]

Proclaiming as he did the originality and independence of Russia, Zhukovsky spoke out against the idea of tsarism's mounting an armed intervention directed against revolutionary Europe: "It seems to me that in this event Providence has clearly indicated both the present duty and the future destiny of Russia: it is a separate world existing according to its own inner laws of development, in itself it is firm and inviolable. Directed toward the outside, the most it can do is to waste its strength and destroy its own edifice in another's calamity."[14]

Throughout the reign of Nicholas I, Zhukovsky, who did not live to see the Crimean War (1853–1856), in his letters to the heir to the throne consistently and categorically warned against any military undertakings whatsoever, on the grounds that they would be dangerous for the Russian autocracy. In this conviction lies the basic pathos of the following lines: "We stand outside all this area which is now convulsed by earthquake; we are strong in our inner strength and rich in our future, but we are strong at home and not outside our own borders. The way of Europe is not our way."[15]

Thus Zhukovsky instructed his "pupil," exploiting to the utmost his opportunity to urge upon him the necessity of abolishing serfdom: "We have as yet no proletarians, we do have *artificial* proletarians [the serfs]; but the government that itself brought them into being can easily destroy them. . . . Russia . . . has now entered on a new period of her existence, a period of the development of *a firm rule of law at home,* a period of the calm acquisition of all the true *treasures of civic life.*"[16] Ten years after Zhukovsky's death, Alexander II, Zhukovsky's pupil, did find it necessary to abolish serfdom in Russia.

VI *End of the Court Appointment. Marriage. Journalism in the 1850's. Translations from the Classic Poets. Death.*

Zhukovsky's career at the court ended in honorable retirement in 1841, when Alexander attained his majority.

A year earlier, while traveling through Europe, Zhukovsky had visited an old friend of his, an artist named Reitern, in Düsseldorf, and had become the object of an ardent infatuation on the part of the artist's daughter, the eighteen-year-old Elizabeth.

He had seen her, long ago, as a little girl, but now, to use his own expression, she "had blossomed out like a rose." The poet's feelings were awakened by the girl's obviously enamored state. It may have seemed to Zhukovsky that here he was faced with a more fortunate variant of a situation similar to the one that had ended so tragically in the past. The young fiancée revived the image of his long-lost Mariya.

Zhukovsky was fifty-eight, his bride eighteen and the marriage did not bring him happiness. Only the first year, it seems, was blissful. The romantic infatuation of the poet's young wife quickly shifted to a black melancholy, the source of which was an unbalanced psychological condition from which she had suffered since childhood. They had children, a boy named Pavel and a girl, Ekaterina. Zhukovsky assumed the entire responsibility for their upbringing. As a result of a fright suffered during an earthquake, his wife's mental condition deteriorated catastrophically. Elizabeth's pathological depression was inherited from her mother's side of the family. In addition, her mother, a follower of one of the more extreme forms of pietism, drew her daughter into the religious atmosphere of that movement. Zhukovsky spent the last twelve years of his life in Germany, for he had to postpone his return to

Russia because of the long cures his wife was undergoing at various German spas. Her illness was the reason for the poet's weary separation from his country, which was to become permanent.

Still, over the last years of his life the poet had his happy moments. They were surely the exceptions, however. A corner of the veil drawn over his private life is lifted in some of his letters to his old friend Zeydlits, a doctor from whom Zhukovsky had no secrets, and to Ekaterina Afanasevna Protasova, Masha's mother, who had played such a fateful part in his life. "Pray to God for us!" Zhukovsky wrote to Ekaterina Protasova in 1847. "Ask above all that I should be given patience." "There are times when I want to knock my head against the wall", he wrote once to Zeydlits.[17]

The strange "program" of family unhappiness which seems to have been "scheduled" at the beginning of Zhukovsky's life worked itself out to the end. Even so, Zhukovsky never allowed his despair and vexation however profound, to spill over into the sphere of generalization. The poet looked upon them as something in the nature of the first step of a ladder. He adopted the Christian doctrine of long-suffering as the cornerstone of his ethical structure: it was this doctrine that defined his public as well as his private ideal. Zhukovsky transformed his family circumstances into a philosophical premise for questions of a general nature. In his later letters, one thought figures constantly: family life is the model of man's lot on earth, given him from above both for his delight and for the tempering and testing of his soul.

To these concepts which had long been natural to Zhukovsky, he added, in his later years, certain features of German pietism, an intensely mystic form of Protestantism that emphasized the need for personal repentance and salvation, often at the expense of the strict Lutheran dogma against which it had originally been a reaction. The influence led him to excessive religious exaltation; somber thoughts on sin and retribution weighed heavily on his spirit. Zhukovsky's friend and biographer, Karl Zeydlits, writes with great disapproval of the unavoidable influence of the society of which the poet had, whether he wanted to or not, become a part, and of the gloomy circumstances of his personal life. Contact with Russian friends, in view of the limited travel and communications facilities of the time, was reduced to a minimum. Even so, Zhukovsky did maintain an extensive correspondence with Aleksandr Turgenev (who died in

1846), with Gogol, and with the members of the Protasov-Moyer family, as well as with the heir to the throne.

The only one of his contemporaries with whom Zhukovsky remained in fairly regular contact throughout the 1840s was Gogol. Gogol would visit Zhukovsky, but he was himself on the verge of mental illness—haunted by terror, depression, the maniacal consciousness of his own sinfulness, the prophet and preacher. Contact with him would have cheered nobody. To some extent Zhukovsky submitted to his friend's moralistic influence. In the Zhukovsky of this period, we can observe a parallel passion for moralizing, for writing hortatory "essays" covering almost every aspect of human life. In these essays, written in the form of letters or talks, there is much that is interesting and even true, but the very aim of "embracing everything" and the dominating ecclesiasticoascetic point of view gives his thoughts a certain narrowness and abstract quality. This finding is supported by the very titles of these essays. Altogether he wrote more than fifty of them between 1845 and 1850, but the following is a fair selection of titles: "Truth," "Faith," "Providence," "Law and Sin," "Science," "Freedom," "Misfortune," "Hope," "The Idea of Being," "Flesh-Spirit," "Public Order," "Censorship," "Discipline," "Despotism," "Autocracy," "A Few Words on the Subject of Ghosts," "On the Death Penalty." The dominant spirit here is one of moralizing pietism. "On Capital Punishment" was particulary disliked, both by contemporaries and future generations. What is astonishing in it is not so much its content (Zhukovsky was protesting against the pointless theatricality of public executions), as the poet's premise that capital punishment as such is unavoidable. The article was clearly written under the influence of Prosper Mérimée's "Mateo Falcone," which he had just translated. The poet suggested that executions should be conducted according to an almost medieval, church ritual; his entire attention is concentrated on "saving the soul" of the criminal.

The poetic works of Zhukovsky written during the last two decades of his life were not, strictly speaking, very important for their day. Not only did they cease to exercise a decisive influence on Russian literature, they even intentionally assumed a position outside it. After "The Prisoner of Chillon," which set the standard for the Russian Romantic narrative poem, and *The Maid of Orleans*, which did the same for drama in verse, Zhukovsky no longer looked for inspiration to the leading works of contemporary Western literature. This, of course, was deliberate policy. He was particularly attracted by the "eternal" creations of human genius, the significance of which had been proven independent of time. Romantic fantasy and mysticism were as dear to him as before, but they also served him now as a convention through which he discovered certain eternal psychological conflicts and human feelings. Of *Undine*, Belinsky wrote: "It is an inexhaustible source of wonder to us how successfully the poet has mingled the world of imagination with the real world and how many sacred secrets of the heart he has managed to display and express in such a fantastic tale."[18] The world of the romantic and the miraculous was not, in Zhukovsky's eyes, the creation of any definite epoch. He looked upon it as a world eternally true to its own laws and equally relevant to people of any age. In 1830, and particularly in 1840, Zhukovsky was a religious Utopian, and this diverted his work from the main course of the Russian literature of that time, where a new poetry and a new prose were developing at breakneck speed.

Zhukovsky's sense of alienation from the modern world found only oblique expression in his poetry, emerging rather in his interest in the ancient world. From 1842 to 1848, the poet worked on, and completed, that translation of the *Odyssey* of which Gogol said that in it "our nineteenth century will detect a powerful reproach to itself." To Zhukovsky, as to Gogol, the ancient world seemed to represent an ideal of harmony, greatness, and nobility of heart; and it was those qualities which Zhukovsky stressed in his *Odyssey* as in his *Nâla and Damayânti*.

In the last years of his life, Zhukovsky found writing poetry increasingly burdensome. Though almost blind, he did not abandon his creative plans. Among the relics of his projects are the fragments of the unfinished *Wandering Jew (Vechnyi zhid)*, in which the poet planned to show the gradual conversion of Ahasuerus to the Christian faith and to the charity of the Gospel.

Zhukovsky had always desired to be a poet who was "a comforter in life," beginning with the early "Teon and Eskhin," with its formula that life sends us all things for good reason, that "sorrow and joy are the means to one end," right through to his later epic poems. The world of Zhukovsky's poetry, while by no means the idyll of a wishful thinker, is nevertheless sealed off from "current" problems, from the passions and sufferings engendered by historical circumstance.

On April 12, 1852, Zhukovsky died in Baden-Baden. In accordance with his wish, the poet's body was taken to Russia to be buried in his native soil.

CHAPTER 2

The Lyric and The Soul

I The Principles of Zhukovsky's Lyricism

ZHUKOVSKY is credited with the aphorism: "With us, a writer of genius might achieve more than Peter the Great!" As we have seen, the poet attached exceptional importance to the content, the aim of art. "Poetry is virtue"; "the poet's words are his deeds"; "poetry should influence the soul of the whole people": these phrases expressed Zhukovsky's understanding of the aims of literature as aims of a primarily moral nature.[1]

From the very beginning this attitude defined Zhukovsky's particular position among the poets who had begun writing at the same time as he. It distinguished Zhukovsky from the elegant epicureanism of his friend and contemporary Konstantin Batyushkov; from the "wild" "Hussar's" muse of the poet partisan, Denis Davydov; from the libertine poetry of the younger Vyazemsky. The best of these poets, Batyushkov, whose talent may be compared with Zhukovsky's own, represented that hedonistic, erotic tradition of eighteenth-century poetry which enjoyed a particularly luxuriant flowering in France. Batyushkov's "pagan" epicureanism, the civic enthusiasm of Davydov and Vyazemsky (and, later, of the Decembrist poets), contrast directly with Zhukovsky's Christian self-denial.

> I see the castles of the rich
> With gardens girt around . . .
> But my road is another which
> Leads me where care is found.
> Yet of good fortune I'm not shy,
> I keep my grief apart;
> Bidding the gay—as I go by—
> "God speed you!" from my heart . . .
>
> ("The Song of the Poor Man," I, 273)

Zhukovsky was a logical and uncompromising thinker. For Batyushkov, with his harmonious, aesthetic ideal, life was acceptable only as a blaze of beauty and happiness, opposed to destruction and despair. Batyushkov's poetry is not without dissonances, the bitter awareness of a life passing irretrievably. Zhukovsky's poetry is a poetry of reconciliation, of the dissolution of man in a world that is full of the breath of the Divinity. It is not surprising that Zhukovsky was so struck by Gogol's phrase that art is "reconciliation with life." Zhukovsky always strove to create a harmonious, lofty, specifically poetic world, firmly rooted in the Ideal, a world in which such human moral concepts as "virtue," "truth," "greatness," and "beauty" were expressed in sublimated form. For him, "the good" and "the beautiful" were inseparable.

Zhukovsky's poetry, like his life, was far from idyllic. Naively idealistic notes are to be found only in his very earliest poems (even in some of his masterpieces, such as the "Village Churchyard" and "Evening"). On the whole, however, Zhukovsky's poetry provides us profound insight into the complexity of human experience, man's striving after the moral and aesthetic ideal, and his sorrow at the awareness of the imperfection of a life "where all, my friend, is victim or destroyer" ("To Turgenev, In Answer to His Letter") (I, 180). Given this choice, Zhukovsky perferred the role of victim. The sadness which pervades his lyric poetry and almost all his work is invariably colored by an element of self-limitation, self-denial.

Zhukovsky remained aloof from the spirit of Romantic individualism which affected his contemporaries in varrying degree. Nothing in him responded either to vividly expressed "demonism" or to the milder forms of individualism in poetry.

The principal feature of Zhukovsky's artistic manner was his lyricism. It would be incorrect to say that his poetry, for all its concentration on feelings and experiences, was psychological in the sense that the poetry of Pushkin, Lermontov, Baratynsky or Tyutchev was psychological. The image of the poet in Zhukovsky's poetry is still somewhat abstract, devoid of individual or psychological features. Yet the atmosphere of poetic, lofty lyricism is a typical characteristic not only of his poetry as a whole, but also of each separate work.

The principle of the poetic "confession" is alien to Zhukovsky's artistic manner. He prefers a summarized description of his emotion to analysis, dissection, or detailed description. But the lyric tenor of every image, of every poetic word serves to enlarge the perspective of the content, semantically enriching the imagery. A special hidden emotionalism—natural to lyricism, as a genre of the art of the word, and differing essentially from the more "open," more obvious emotions of the epic and drama—is particularly characteristic of Zhukovsky's style. It is this trait that invests his poetry with the unfading enchantment and power of the highest flights of poetry.

Zhukovsky uses words in such a way as to render them capacious, rich in implications and associations. Zhukovsky did much to bestow upon the word that wealth of profound association which distinguishes the word as employed in poetry from the same word used in prose.[2]

This multisignificance is rooted in Zhukovsky's understanding of the complex relationships of man with the world around him. Since the days of Petrarch, the problem of "man and the world" has been understood throughout European lyric poetry as the problem of "man and culture." This concept, of course, had its origins in the remote past and, in Zhukovsky's poetry (as also, incidentally, in Petrarch's), is closely linked with his conception of the divine "creation" of nature. Hence the veneration of nature so especially characteristic of Zhukovsky.

"We would overlook one of Zhukovsky's most important features," wrote Belinsky, "if we failed to mention that poet's divine gift for describing scenes from nature and imbuing them with romantic life."[3] Among Zhukovsky's lyric verses we will scarcely find one in which the lyrical subject is not developed against the background of a landscape. Even the word "background" is misleading. It does not convey the essence of Zhukovsky's manner, by which the world (the landscape, the natural setting) and man are always presented in a kind of unity.

Zhukovsky was the first Russian poet to introduce not only the colors, sounds, and smells of nature into his work (all of which helps form its "material" charm), but also, as it were, to endow nature with the thoughts and feelings of the human beings who view it. This concept constitutes the basic framework (despite all the differences between them) of such poems as "The Village Churchyard," "Evening," "Slavyanka," "A Sentiment of Spring," "Desire" ("Zhelanie"), "To the Moon" ("K mesyatsu"), "The Inexpressible" ("Nevyrazimoe"), "The Moth and the Flowers" ("Motylyok i tsvety"), and many other masterpieces of Zhukovsky's lyric poetry.

Let us first examine the original elegy "Evening" (1806), which has received a generous share of critical study by scholars, but which still remains a never-failing source of appreciative enthusiasm on the part of the reader:

> Already evening . . . and the clouds' bright rims
> Have faded. On high towers the last ray slowly dies,
> The last faint-gleaming ripple on the river dims
> And flickers out beneath dulled skies.
>
> All's quiet; trees sleep sound; around me all is still,
> And, stretched out on the grass beneath a bending willow,
> I hear the chuckling haste of a leaf-hidden rill
> To mingle with the river's shallows.
>
> How mingled with the cool the incense of the leaves!
> How sweet in stillness here to listen to the river!
> How quietly o'er the waters wafts the soft-blown breeze
> The supple willow branches quiver!
>
> (I, 47)

In the first verse quoted here, the dominant words are all colored by a similar emotional mood: "have faded," "last," "dies," "last," "dulled," "flickers out". Yet Zhukovsky does not resort to simple—positive or negative—parallelism in his evocation of nature and man. In the second verse, where the poet depicts himself, the dominant words are emotionally neutral, almost prosaic: "stretched out," "bending," "I hear," "chuckles," "to mingle." In this way the poet is neither brought into too close contact with the fading landscape, nor set at too great a distance from it. And in this way, too, the state of contemplation, of meditation, is expressed not only thematically ("stretched out . . . I hear"), but also by the very character of the words employed. A profound emotion infects the reader and renders him, as it were, a participant in the creative act.

The words in this elegy have more than one level of meaning; they include an objective meaning and a psychological meaning (melancholy). In the Russian original, there is a deliberate, musical use of assonance in *pomerknuli-poslednii*, *luch-potukhshii*, and in the semantically and morphologically homogeneous rhymes *umiraet-ugasaet*. The beauty, the poetic worth of the words also become a part of their content. The semantics of these words however, are somewhat loose: Zhukovsky is not seeking precision or differentiation. Through this multiple meaningfulness and associative evocativeness he achieves an effect of things left unsaid, of spacious scope for possible reinterpretation. Zhukovsky's use of words is remarkable for this ability to leave his reader in possession of a *semantic reserve*.

Owing to the "deliberate complexity of meaning" in his use of words,[4] Zhukovsky is able to convey the deepest stirrings of the heart. For instance, the stillness in the poem "Evening" is at once a real stillness and a stillness of the heart. Later it would become one of the poet's favorite images. It is not "dying" or "fading," but this complex image of "stillness" that provides, in this elegy, the link between man and nature. To depict a state of being harmoniously at one with the natural world is undoubtedly a part of Zhukovsky's basic concept. Even the twice-repeated use of the word *slivat'sia* ("to mingle") contributes to this impression: the little rill "mingles" with the river, and the scent of growing things is "mingled" with the cool of evening in the famous line "How mingled with the cool the incense of the leaves."

Just as complex and semantically weighted is the epithet "sweet." Zhukovsky was the first poet in Russian literature to make wide use of it in the psychological, Petrarchan sense (*dolce*). The "sweetness" of the contemplation of nature as a material expression of the beauty of this present life is, for Zhukovsky, a most important aspect of the life of the soul, not only in "Evening," but in many other works as well (e.g., "Sentiment of Spring," "Slavyanka," and "To the Moon").

The lyrical emotionalism found in Zhukovsky's lyric poetry has much in common with music. Perhaps no other Russian poet's work was so organically connected with music. The room Zhukovsky always left for "unexpressed" associations creates an inner connection with the principles of the art of music, a connection confirmed by "exterior" elements.

In Zhukovsky's poetry, a particularly significant place is occupied by the song, the romance. Many of his poems are actually called "Song": these include "My Friend, My Guardian Angel," "O, Dearest Friend! Now Thou Art Joyful," "The Charm of Days Gone By." If we comprehend Zhukovsky's conscious use of music to lend greater expressiveness to his verse, we will understand the great significance of sound-painting in Zhukovsky's poetic method, the composition of many of his verses (the use of couplets, refrains, etc.), and, finally, the actual way in which he uses words. "The

whole of Nature was a song to me"—these words from the introduction to *Undine* do not, of course, refer in any literal sense to what
we have been saying, but they do reveal a great deal about
Zhukovsky's poetry.

In his verse Zhukovsky pays much attention to the elaboration of
mood. The interrogative approach, another typical characteristic of
the song, is the mood he makes use of most often. In this connection, it is interesting to point out the purely songlike system of
exclamations and exhortations which always lend a characteristic
intonation to Zhukovsky's poetry.[5] It is no wonder his verses have so
often been set to music; for the potentiality of a musical interpretation was already organically contained within them. For example,
the first three lines of the elegy "Evening," set to music by
Tchaikovsky, are immediately recognizable as musically organized,
even if we detach ourselves from the familiar melody. The com-
positional symmetry characteristic of the song and the uniformity of
musical periods here find their counterpart in the pattern of the
exclamations: "kak slit," "kak sladko," "kak tikho" ("how mingled,"
"how sweetly," "how softly"). From the point of view, of sound effects
we perceive clearly the melodic shifts in the accented vowels *i*, *e*,
and *a*, which are sounded successively once again, with increased
emphasis, in the last line: "*I gibkoi ivy trepetan'e*. . . ."

A remarkably rich variety of rhythms distinguishes Zhukovsky's
poetry. It contains the most varied forms and combinations of iambic meter: blank iambic pentameter, hexameter, four-foot iambic
lines with masculine rhymes throughout (a verse form later given
high poetic standing by Lermontov in his narrative poem *Mtsyri*),
the trochee with dactylic endings, not to mention the wide use of
trisyllabic meters (dactyls, amphibrachs, anapests).[6] Use of such a
wide variety of meters enabled Zhukovsky to convey complex
shades of mood and emotion, not only through words and their
meanings, but also phonetically. "What cannot be said in words,
whisper to the soul in sounds"—these words, by which Afanasy Fet
sought to express the essence of his poetry in the poem "No, I've No
Song of Passion for Thee" ("Net, ne zhdi ty pesni strastnoi"), are
equally applicable to Zhukovsky's lyrics.

"Romances" and "songs": thus Zhukovsky himself entitled an
important section of the editions of his collected verse published
during his lifetime. His "songs" include both original and translated
works. It is noteworthy that in some of Zhukovsky's translations the
subtitle "Song" appears when it was not present in the original (cf.,

for example, the subtitle to Zhukovsky's translation of Schiller's "Die Ideale" ["Mechty"]). It is also characteristic of Zhukovsky that he actually transforms the phonetic structure of the verse to make it more songlike; in Schiller's original there is less phonetic symmetry. For example the correspondence between the exclamations in the first and the second lines is lacking.

It is not only the phonetic structure and meter, but also the principle of the construction of an image, the principle of the use of words themselves, which often (but, as we shall seek to demonstrate later, not always) invest Zhukovsky's poetry with its songlike, lyric quality. The word-image in the song possesses its own specific characteristics, and in this field Zhukovsky was a great master. To a certain extent, his achievement stemmed from his association with the tradition of sentimental songwriting and poetry of the late eighteenth and early nineteenth centuries; Nikolay Lvov, Yury Neledinsky-Meletsky, and Ivan Dmitriev may be cited. This association was particularly noticeable in the poetry written between 1800 and the early 1810s. Their songlike quality here assumes a conventionalized elegiac form:

> When that I was beloved, in ecstasies, in pleasure,
> The days of life flowed by like an enchanting dream.
>
> (I, 45)

Later, the "musicality" of Zhukovsky's poetry attained ever greater perfection, while remaining the basic element of his lyricism. This development sprang from that generalized descriptive quality of his use of words which we have already mentioned.

The vital words of Zhukovsky's poetic lexicon are those conveying general, rather than individual, emotions, for instance "memory," "sorrow," "joy," "stillness," "life," "love." But in Zhukovsky's poetry these words have several dimensions of meaning. Possessed of great "reserves" of significance, they call up a whole chain of associations that lead into the very depths of man's emotional life. This type of word-image, closely akin to music, in many ways defines the specific grace of Zhukovsky's lyricism, and is evident not only in his original works, but also in his translations.

As an example, we may quote the poem "To the Moon" (1817):

> Once again the wood and vale
> Drown in misty gleam;

In your stillness sweet my soul
Melts as in a dream.

You appeared—and quietly
Meadows dark grew bright,
As a smile, quite suddenly,
Floods our life with light.

Grief and joy of far-off years
Echo back to me,
In the stillness I can hear
Call of memory.

Down, my stream, go gushing by!
Life has lost its bloom;
So my hopes went rushing by
So my love is gone. . . .

(I, 289–90)

Here, no single word suggests any sharply individual shade of meaning in "sorrow" and "joy"; yet the torrent of emotional "information" released by these lines is very powerful.

The opening chord for the entire poem is the phrase "Once again." Placed as it is at the very beginning, in the position where it will assume the greatest possible metric weight, it acquires a heightened semantic intensity, expressing the resurrection of a past experience of the heart. In this way, the poem's time setting is enlarged to include what happened long ago.

"To the Moon" is a translation of a poem by Goethe of the same title, "An den Mond," in which the emotions are clearly defined and depicted in more detail. In Goethe's poem, for all the melancholy that pervades it, the dominant mood is one of calm, even as the moon's gaze is "calming" to the poet. From the beginning, Goethe is concerned with the elegiac problem of the impossibility of recalling the past. Zhukovsky, however, does recall this past, to experience once again with full intensity the sorrow of his loss (he hears "an echo" and "a salutation" from bygone days). The soul is wide open to impressions from the past. Goethe, in this same passage, speaks of bidding farewell to the past and even of finding release from it. Zhukovsky does not diminish the original: he simply creates different images.

In the Russian word *rastvoril* ("melted") we again discover the multiplicity of meaning so characteristic of the Russian poet. One of

the word's meanings is "opened," but the basic idea is connected
with Zhukovsky's concept of the mingling of the "inner" and the
"outer," of the "dissolving" of the one in the other. As in "Evening,"
"sweet stillness" is once again both stillness in nature and a state of
the soul. It is not so much the expression "sweet stillness" as such as
the fact that it opens or "dissolves" the soul (*rastvoriaet dushu*); this
is the great discovery of Zhukovsky as lyric poet, all the greater for
the fact that he is translating no less a poet than Goethe.

One of the specific characteristics of Zhukovsky's lyric poetry is
his talent for investing conventional literary themes with life and
conviction. He varies and combines the same themes, reworking
them into complete, original compositions. Thus "times gone by"
(*minuvshee*) is one of Zhukovsky's favorite word-themes.[7] He is
always looking back to the past. But this conventional, almost banal,
theme of elegiac poetry achieves in his poetry, as we have seen,
profound emotional significance.

In Zhukovsky's poetry, words are oriented toward evocation of
emotional *experience*, not of new and untried sensations. This orientation is also reminiscent of the principles of classical music.

The word "chord" used earlier is a common enough metaphor,
but it is singularly apt when applied to Zhukovsky's style. The
musical organization of the line cited above and of those that followed it is of a very high caliber. In them, as in "Evening," are
dominant full-voiced, melodious passages of ringing sound. In the
first verse, the harmonious diphthongs (the "*i*-vowels") occur within
both the rhymes, and, in each case, also preceding the rhymes:
tumannyi tvoi; *sladkoi tishinoi*. The monosyllabic words *les*, *dol*,
and *blesk* emphasize by way of contrast the long-drawn-out
tumannyi. *Les* and *blesk* are assonances.

This vividly expressed phonetic musicality has a function of
meaning, for it creates a more immediate and convincing sense of
real experience.

II *The Measure of Subjectivism. The Lyrical Hero.*
Special Features of Zhukovsky's Romanticism.

Zhukovsky once asked: "What else is art but a copy of life and the
world made with all the fidelity of which our seeing and understanding souls are capable?" ("On Melancholy in Life and in Poetry").[8] At first sight these words might be taken as those of an ex-

treme subjectivist. If, however, we analyze them more carefully, the poet's words turn out to have objective significance.

It would, of course, be idle to pretend that Zhukovsky was altogether free from subjectivism. Certain features of subjectivism were present in all European literature of the eighteenth century: in the works of the Sentimentalists, the Sturm und Drang, the Pre-romantics. In Russia, this special characteristic attained its most vivid expression in the school of Karamzin. Here subjectivism had not yet become a principle of perceiving and even of distorting the world, a criterion of artistic imagery, but was used rather to add color to it. Zhukovsky's plaintive, gentle lyricism, the generalized style of his songs, created a singleness of tone and defined the poet's individuality. Lyricism, however, is not identical with individualism.

If we compare the editions of Zhukovsky in which his poetry is classified according to genre (as Zhukovsky himself elected to publish it), and those editions in which a chronological arrangement has been preferred, we will see that Zhukovsky paid attention to genre categories. For instance, if we read his verses of the year 1814 one after another in the sequence in which they were written, we will obtain no comprehensive impression of the poet and his inner life. The melancholy verses on love and separation contrast sharply with the letters to Aleksandr Voeykov, to Turgenev, to Alexander I, with "Teon and Eskhil," and with the jesting "Dolbino letters" (written in the village of Dolbino on the estate of Zhukovsky's friends who took him in after the quarrel with Ekaterina Protasova). The section "1814" does not convey to the reader the smallest inkling that this was the saddest year of Zhukovsky's life, full of tragic events and bitter disappointments in his hopeless struggle for personal happiness. To explain the variety of Zhukovsky's poetic genres by variations in the mood of the poet or by romantic transitions from one emotional state to another would be to place an impermissibly strained interpretation on his work of this period.

Romantic irony was completely alien to Zhukovsky: he thought it an almost diabolical mockery of things sacred. In his jesting letters we find, not irony, which always implies a sliding scale of values, but pure humor: jesting a little with his friends provides relief from lofty thoughts and suffering, but at no point do the two intersect.

In his lyric poetry, Zhukovsky was always careful to sublimate the raw material of life. More often than not, he conveys "the story" of his life through traditional lyrical subjects and situations. In so doing, he transforms the all but mortal anguish and despair through which he had passed: the very literariness, the aestheticism of the images he created made them objects of contemplation, a contemplation that afforded relief. The earliest lyrics in which Zhukovsky utilized the subject clichés of Sentimentalism were particularly literary in quality. The traditional image of the Sentimental bard, suffering from unhappy love and full of premonitions of his own early death, may be found in "Longing for the Beloved" and many other poems. In an adaptation of some verse excerpts from *Don Quixote* (not Cervantes' *Quixote*, but an adaptation by Jean Pierre Claris de Florian) Zhukovsky presents the lover's sonnet in the spirit of a sentimental pastoral.

In his magnificent poem "The Bard" Zhukovsky took a ready-made subject and established a new standard for the poetry of Russian Sentimentalism:

> He sang of friendship, but his friend so true,
> A friendly hand in his, did wither in his prime.
> He sang of Love—but sorrowful his rhyme.
> Alas! Love's torments and nought else he knew.
>
> (I, 110)

"He sang of friendship," "sang of love," "withered in his prime"—these are all typical stock phrases of sentimental poetry. Yet what acute anguish lies behind them: the loss of his dearest friend and an unusual love story, whose principals found themselves, through no fault of their own, in a situation of tragic conflict.

"The Bard" (like other poems of the same kind) is so conceived as to preclude any identification of the "poet" with the image of the author; the bard, his grave, his external appearance, and his inner world as portrayed in this poem unite to form a picture that has its own independent existence. It is as though the author were painting this picture for his reader at one remove from what he is actually depicting.

> Beneath the trees, above the limpid waters,
> Do you not see yon mound of turf, my friends?
>
> (I, 109)

"The Bard," like many other poems by Zhukovsky (particularly of
the early period), has a "lyrical hero," a connecting link between the
poet's spiritual world and its expression. Zhukovsky's lyrical hero is
remembered both by his contemporaries and by posterity. He is
easily distinguished by the literary conventionality of his characteristics. He is at once author and *persona*, whose typical features
(thoughtfulness and melancholy) have been predetermined by the
requirements of the elegiac genre. His fate (unhappy love and early
death) is similarly predetermined:

> He was a simple soul, a tender spirit,
> But, in this world, a pilgrim of one day;
> Scarce grown to prime—he longed to be away
> Perceiving in this life but little merit.
> And soon, indeed, he met his end;
> His life was brief—so brief, so hard,
> He met death as a welcome friend,
> Poor bard!
>
> (I, 110)

The expression "lyrical hero" is often used in a broader sense to
apply to all aspects of the author's image in poetry. It is also used in
the analysis of subjective poetry, which concentrates particularly on
communicating the personal character and destiny of the author.
Some scholars consider the term unnecessary and conducive to a
lack of clarity in the analysis of a lyrical work; yet it undoubtedly
helps us to differentiate between the various kinds of self-expression
in the work of a lyrical author.[9] It serves its purpose best when the
poet is not striving for an effect of spontaneous lyrical "confession,"
but when there is a consciously elaborated and polished image of the
author, a kind of *persona*. The convention of the lyrical hero focuses
attention on the psychology and destiny of the poet; yet at the same
time it draws a veil over his individuality. He is put together,
constructed by the poet in just the same way as are the heroes of the
epic or drama.

Goethe, with the other, spontaneous type of lyric verse in mind,
remarked that every poem is "occasional verse." For the lyrical hero
the "occasion" is often an imaginary one. Of the poets of standing
among Zhukovsky's contemporaries Batyushkov and Davydov both
created lyrical heroes: Batyushkov in the antique *persona* of his

"Bacchante," "Elysium," and other poems, Davydov in his image of the poet-Hussar.

The lyrical hero is always a personification of certain of the poet's own concepts. As a *persona*, his role is that of the object described rather than that of the describing subject. It is thus in the natural order of things that Zhukovsky's "Village Churchyard" should end with a depiction of the imagined grave of the poet himself, seen and described by a chance witness, a "villager":

> Here all untimely buried lie the young man's ashes,
> Nor fame nor fortune knew he in this world below,
> And yet the Muses never turned away their faces
> And Melancholy's sacred seal was on his brow.
>
> (I, 33)

Thus, in the finale of the "Village Churchyard," the author relegates himself to the third person: the pronoun "I" is replaced by the pronoun "he." In the same way, in the elegy "Evening," the author's "I" is, in the conclusion, again replaced by the word "youth." The poet speaks of himself as of one of the *dramatis personae* of his poem, depicting himself from the outside:

> To sing, then, is my lot . . . for long? . . . How can I tell?
> Ah! Soon perhaps Alpin will hither come at evening
> With sad Minvana, here to wish the youth farewell,
>   And by his quiet grave sit dreaming!
>
> (I, 49)

Gradually Zhukovsky outgrew the most obvious clichés of Sentimentalist poetry. In his mature works, they stand out as an anachronism, as a leftover from a discarded manner, set off from the rest of his own work by their archaic impact.

If, as in "The Village Churchyard," this style is delimited by, and wholly corresponds to, the content of the elegy, in the concluding lines of "Evening" it already seems somewhat old-fashioned in comparison with the style of the poem as a whole.

In the period of the most intensive development of his lyric verse, after 1811, Zhukovsky makes less use of the lyrical hero and cultivates other forms of self-expression.

To purely Sentimental motifs the poet added certain Preromantic conventions. In European, late eighteenth-century literature, Pre-

romanticism and Sentimentalism are extremely close, and often
overlapping, but never merging tendencies. In Russia from the very
beginning they were conjoined in the work of Karamzin and his·
followers. Sentimentalism emphasized a cult of nature, sensitivity,
and virtue, coupled with interest in the intimate "life of the heart,"
whereas preromanticism utilized the fantastic, the folk element, the
exotic, the medieval, the poetry of "mystery and horror," among
other things. Zhukovsky did not simply follow in Karamzin's footsteps but was himself strongly influenced by Western preromanticism and developed along the lines it had prescribed. His preromanticism first found expression in his ballads, and subsequently diffused into his lyric poetry.

Thus in the elegy "Slavyanka" (1815) a strange feeling of mystery
permeates the sentimental description of "fading nature," which
calls to the poet's mind the melancholy symbol of a memorial urn.
The young birch trees rear up before the wayfarer like a specter and
the enchanted stillness is haunted by some invisible presence:

> A face without a form, a misted gaze at one
> With wreathing mists of midnight darkness . . .

>   (I, 264)

The question of the "degree" or "type" of Zhukovsky's Romanticism is arguable and has remained to this day a subject of scholarly
controversy. It is an important question, for whatever degree of
maturity Zhukovsky achieved in Romantic style and method, there
can be no doubt about his central importance in preparing and
developing this literary trend in Russia.

Even during the poet's lifetime, several different opinions were
expressed on his connection with Romanticism. Nikolay Polevoy
considered that the poet "had hardly had time to catch and analyze
one of the rays which Romanticism sent shining forth over
Europe."[10] Belinsky, in his articles on Pushkin, proclaimed
Zhukovsky the founder of Russian Romanticism.

In his well-known monograph on Zhukovsky, Academician Veselovsky maintains that the poet never in fact emerged completely
from the mold of Sentimentalism. He based his study of Zhukovsky
on examples of his coolly intellectual conception of man: Zhukovsky
displayed, he says, "so much dreaminess and self-observation, so
many impulses toward the heavenly heights—and so much love for
pedagogic timetables."[11]

In his book *Pushkin and the Russian Romantics*, G. A. Gukovsky interprets Zhukovsky as a profoundly Romantic poet. Basing his arguments on Zhukovsky's love of "indefinite" and imprecise words ("something," "it seems," "inexplicable," etc.), and seeing them as the expression of the wavering mistiness of the poet's own apprehension of reality, the critic finds Zhukovsky's impressionism subjectively alogical and unmotivated.

However, behind what Zhukovsky is saying there is always the concept of some eternal, mysterious essence of the world. It does not "vex the eye with artificial brightness" (the phrase is Fet's), but it is completely objective.

In his elegy "Slavyanka," such favorite expressions of Zhukovsky's as "I think," "it seems," "someone," are all objectively motivated. They depict a vision that appeared to the poet "in reality" and raised the curtain upon a world of mystery:

> And someone by this urn is sitting silently
> And—so it seems to me—he stares dark-eyed upon me . . .
>
> (I, 360)

In the poem "Lalla Rookh," where the atmosphere of mystery is particularly heavy ("It seems," "dream, the captor of the soul") the conception of "two worlds" is developed, and the poet hymns "the herald" of the higher world of true reality: "the spirit of pure beauty" ("genii chistoi krasoty," in Zhukovsky's formula, later immortalized by Pushkin):

> Fleeting are his visitations
> Coming when our being is pure;
> And he bringeth revelations
> Troubled hearts and minds to cure;
> That the heart might know of heaven
> In this dark, terrestial sphere,
> Sometimes he will grant us even
> A glimpse beyond the veil—to there.
>
> (I, 360)

In "Lalla Rookh" we have a clear statement of Zhukovsky's philosophy of life and of the relationship in which his poetry stands to Romanticism.

The Romantic idea of the world evolved as a reaction against the conception of the world and man developed during the age of enlightenment. Its distinguishing feature is dualism. The individual and the world about him are conceived of as being catastrophically out of touch. In European literatures of the nineteenth century, even after due allowance has been made for the conceptual variety within the Romantic movement, it is possible to distinguish two main trends. One is the "individualistic," which may also be called the Byronic. The core of this type of Romanticism is the individual personality and the protest of the individual against a hostile environment. Here dualism finds its expression in the hopeless conflict between the freedom-loving, restless, frequently demonic hero and the "prosaic" society to which he is opposed.

In the other branch of Romanticism (particularly well developed in German literature), the main focus of attention is not the individual personality but the surrounding world, which is represented as being beyond human comprehension. Here it is the world itself which appears dual, for behind its apparent phenomena a mysterious essence is concealed. And here, too, the dualism manifests itself not so much in the conflict between the individual and society as in the *philosophical concept of the duality of the world*.

Thus, individualism and its corollary, subjectivism, are intrinsic features not so much of Romanticism as a whole as of one particular, "personalistic" branch of Romanticism. To this branch Zhukovsky was alien. It was hence only natural that he remained aloof from Byron's influence and never accepted Lermontov.

Zhukovsky was a Preromantic whose development led him toward the second, preeminently German type of romanticism.

The duality of his conception of the world found expression in the contrasting of the religious concepts of "heaven" and "earth," often given form in extremely complex structures of artistic ideas.

The concept of a dual world pervades the poem "Slavyanka" and other works of the same year, 1815: "The Roses are Blooming" ("Rozy rastsvetaiut"), "The Singing-Bird" ("Ptichkoi pevitsoi"), "Eastward, Ever Eastward" ("K vostoku, vsë k vostoku"), and others. As a Preromantic. Zhukovsky saw nature as animated, possessed of a "soul," with which his own soul might commune.

> With thrilling heart I come beneath these hallowed eaves,
> And in this stillness I detect a voice of greeting;
> As though ethereal being were wafting through the leaves,
>   And the invisible were breathing;

As though concealed beneath the bark of these young trees,
Through this enchanted stillness welcome sound dispersing,
A voice, a soul unseen were reaching out to me
      And with this soul of mine conversing . . .

(I, 264)

In "Slavyanka" the images are bolder than in the earlier "Evening," with its traditionally sentimental ending featuring the melancholy singer ("To sing, then, is my lot . . . ," etc.). Here it is not the coolness that mingles with a scent, but a "soul unseen" that diffuses itself in the "enchanted stillness." This image is far more profound than the purely rational concepts of Sentimentalism. Twenty years after this poem Tyutchev was to write:

No plaster-mask, no soulless visage;
Nature is not as you suppose . . .
She has a soul, a tongue to speak with,
And she knows love, and freedom knows.

(Tyutchev, I, 245)

Tyutchev's Romantic concept of the "world soul" was far removed from Zhukovsky's artless faith. Nevertheless, there is a direct line of descent from the magnificent image of the soul, concealed beneath the bark, to Tyutchev.

"Slavyanka" and the "Songs" of 1815 were followed by "Sentiment of Spring," "The Flower of the Covenant," "To a Passing Genius of my Acquaintance" ("K mimo proletevshemu znakomomu geniiu"), "The Inexpressible," "Lalla Rookh," "The Ghost" ("Prividenie"), "The Mysterious Guest" ("Tainstvennyi posetitel' "), and "The Moth and the Flowers." This last poem, written in 1824, marked the end of Zhukovsky's original lyric work. In "The Moth and the Flowers," we see clearly the way Zhukovsky combines a certain obviousness in his religious and moral didacticism with boldness of Romantic insight into the secret "life" and significance of nature. "The Moth and the Flowers" is a triumph of Zhukovsky's Romanticism. Pushkin, who was so foreign to misty idealism, assessed the lofty significance of these verses most positively.

Not born to give consideration
To sentiments you cannot know,

We seek you without expectation
And without grief we let you go.

Then yield you to the wanton breeze's motion
Which is—as you—but moment'ry.
A different charm commands the moth's devotion . . .
Small herald of eternity.

(I, 370)

In the literature on Zhukovsky, much space is devoted to the poetic and philosophical sources from which he derived and sustained his Romantic ideas. The most important of these were the works of Kant, Fichte, and Novalis. Nevertheless, Zhukovsky remained aloof from the extremes of Romantic idealism. He disapproved of Ludwig Tieck because the latter's thoughts were based more on imagination than on essential reality. Neither was he particularly close to the Russian "lovers of wisdom" (*liubomudry*). Although, in 1832, he defended Ivan Kireevsky's journal, *The European* (*Evropeets*), which had been banned in government circles, he was in fact remarkably indifferent to the philosophical program of the *liubomudry*, although at first sight it would appear to have been calculated to interest him. In 1836, he approved some verses by Tyutchev—intended for publication in Pushkin's *The Contemporary* (*Sovremennik*)—obviously without seeing them as akin to his own poetry; or at least, if he did, we know nothing of it. It seems rather that Zhukovsky simply did not realize that Tyutchev would be a great continuer of his own work, a great poet of Romantic "Naturphilosophie," whose forerunner he himself was.

III   *The Lyric of the State of Soul*

Although never an advocate of "confession," Zhukovsky nevertheless contrived a perfect means of conveying human feeling through poetry. In Zhukovsky's scheme of things, man's place in the world was a very important one. As he saw it, the human mind was an ultrarefined instrument for contact with the outer world in its most varied manifestations, whether the "secret" life of that world not usually immediately apprehensible by man; or signals emanating from this "secret" world—its sounds, scents, colors; or, beyond all this, its "eternal" values of goodness and beauty.

Zhukovsky's poetry does not distinguish between individual characters and feeling. On the contrary, it is remarkable because it constantly evokes and reevokes one and the same "state of soul": inspiration, animation, a controlled but exalted intensity of reaction to the impressions of the exterior world, enabling the subject to penetrate its "mysteries."

This power of evocation is the outstanding feature of Zhukovsky's lyric poetry and one that distinguishes it from the lyricism of Sentimentalism (although the poet was undoubtedly indebted to the latter). Sentimentalism cultivated *mood* and the mature Zhukovsky, *state of soul*, which is not the same thing at all. "Mood" in poetry is a forerunner of subjectivism. It colors the exterior world according to its own whim and thus often deprives it of its independent, material reality.

In this way, Zhukovsky himself introduces into his translation of Gray's "Elegy" such expressions as "grows pale" and "sunk in thought" which we do not find in the original, thereby independently creating the "mood," but at the same time detracting from the real, material detail of the descriptions.

The other form of Zhukovsky's lyricism—the conveyance of a "state of soul"—does not detract from the material quality of descriptions but, on the contrary, presupposes the power of observation and acute reaction to the surrounding world. The realism of Zhukovsky's description of material objects is, of course, quite different from Derzhavin's. Derzhavin describes what can be—and should be—visible to anybody at all times; Zhukovsky, that which is only perceptible through that controlled exaltation of soul which permits the poet to hear the silence being broken by the falling of a leaf, as in the poem "Slavyanka."

In Zhukovsky's languorously landscaped elegies ("The Village Churchyard," "Evening," and, again, "Slavyanka"), there are descriptions of country life abounding in material detail in the spirit of Derzhavin. Naturally, this style was not Zhukovsky's own discovery, although in some contexts it took on a new coloration.

Some of Zhukovsky's insights into the material world are very interesting and complex. Derzhavin saw the way the sky is reflected in the water and the way birds flying in the sky seem to be "flying in the meadow" ("A Walk in Tsarskoe Selo"); he saw the brilliant colors of the banquet table: "green sorrel soup," "glowing red ham" ("To Evgeny. Life at Zvanskoe"); he saw how "through blue veins courses the rosy blood" ("Russian Girls"). All this is materially, sensually

real. Yet the following verses from Zhukovsky cannot be denied a
certain material, sensual reality:

> I walk a winding path beneath the forest eaves;
> Each step—and a new scene is to my eyes unfolding;
> Now, gleaming sudden through the trees, as though all wreathed
>   In smoke—a bright vale I'm beholding.
> Then all is gone again. . . . The forest thickens now;
> Here all is wild and strange, the twilight, and the silence;
> Save when, from time to time, through the dark, vaulted boughs,
>   There steal diurnal shafts of radiance.
> To gild the roots and pallid, thrusting plants with light;
> Save when some breath of wind, a little leaf loose shaking,
> Sends it a-fluttering down, against the dimness bright,
>   So, by its fall, the stillness breaking.
>
> (I, 261)

This sound of a falling leaf, heard by a poet, marked the beginning
of a new era in the Russian lyric. Derzhavin had heard the roar of
the waterfall: "An avalanche of diamonds falls . . ." ("The Waterfall"), but the gleam of the leaf "against the dimness," the sound of
its falling, the sudden ripple on the water, the swan hidden among
the low shrubs and "shining" there—all these were new, real,
material aspects of a world that Zhukovsky was the first "to see."

He applied an analogous technique in describing mountain scen-
ery in his free translation of Goethe's "Der Morgen kam," and of the
moonlit night in his "Inventory of the Moon" ("Podrobnyi otchet o
lune").

> Beneath the drowsy, opiate ray
> The world itself, it seemed, was drowsing—
> Save for the whispering waters' play,
> Save for some day-bird's sleepy rousing,
> Save when, along the empty road,
> His shadow close beside him keeping,
> Belated, some lone traveler strode
> And broke the stillness of the evening.
>
> (I, 353)

As we can see, Zhukovsky did not merely use the concept of
"mist" as a background to emphasize the melancholy mood of the

poet, and his moon is not just "sorrowful and pale." In the moonlit night he saw the shadow of the lonely traveler keeping pace with him along the road and sensed the startled rousing of a sleepy bird.

The monotonous melancholy of sentimental lyricism was predominant in early nineteenth-century poetry, and it did not lend itself to detailed perception of material reality. The range of words used to convey a sustained emotional atmosphere severely limited the scope of things to be described. Pushkin disliked "monotony" in this sense, calling it "uniformity" (for instance, he disliked Lamartine's elegies for their "insupportable uniformity"). But of Zhukovsky he wrote: "No one ever has had or will have a style to equal his power and variety."[12]

The lofty dreaminess of Zhukovsky's verses did not strike Pushkin as "monotonous," precisely because this quality was not felt as an obstacle to a sweeping and penetrating view of the surrounding world. Zhukovsky obtained the effect of unity of the state of soul without resorting to monotony of emotional coloring. He obtained his goal by endowing the very objects he described with *animation*. This animation of outward things is sometimes directly connected with the Romantic conception of nature, but at other times the link is extremely tenuous. In the poem "The Light Has Dawned" ("Vzoshla zaria . . ."), the mist "flies up" like a live being, the mist is "winged." In the same poem, the breath of dawn is said to have "lured" sleep away.

> And day had sprung, a fiery-winged Spirit!
> And to the living heart all things were living.
>
> (I, 338)

The general "aliveness" of nature, in which man is organically included—such is the Romantic concept, and a most fruitful one it is for poetry.

All these "leaves" of Zhukovsky's are alive, "stirring." Typical in this respect is the epithet in "a sleepy leaf is stirring" ("Slavyanka"). Zhukovsky's feeling for the "aliveness" of living creatures was particularly intense (let us once more recall the way Zhukovsky, in all the vast world of life, notices one tiny creature—the sleepy bird aroused). His swan is not merely observed from without as a "shining" object, but it has "hidden" in the bushes. Here we have at one and the same time a remarkable refinement of the poetic "instrument" and a profound sympathy with all living things, not only in the Romantic but also in the more everyday sense of the word. This refinement and sensitivity explain why these elements of Zhukovsky's poetry were adopted by Pushkin and by Russian poetry after him.

The peculiar emotional quality of Zhukovsky's poetry is intimately linked with the foregoing observations. His poetry is characterized not only by the melancholy reflectiveness of Sentimentalism, but by something else as well: exaltation of soul, inspiration, an awakened consciousness, swift to record and to interpret all it sees. Pushkin, for all the distance separating him from Zhukovsky, seems to be restating in his own words the fundamental experience of the latter's poetry in "The Prophet":

> And then I heard the sky gongs stricken,
> And angels soaring in the height,
> And monsters move through ocean night,
> And vines in mountain-valleys quicken.
>
> (Pushkin, III, 30)

The elegy "Slavyanka" is one of Zhukovsky's most remarkable poems along these lines. Here the poetry is extremely rich, and this richness it owes above all to its awareness of the external world, perceived through an acutely sensitive human consciousness. In "Slavyanka," Zhukovsky interweaves in a single, complex whole his impressions of the countryside, his dreams of glory and the fatherland, sorrowful memories and astonishingly sharp-eyed observations. The picture he paints of the visible, external world is at once poeticized and extraordinarily accurate.

> And here a church is glimpsed through birch with maple twining;
> And there a swan, safe-hidden on the shrub-grown bank,
> Stands still amid the dimness shining.
>
> (I, 263)

Through this combination of thoughts, observations, and emotions, through this sensitivity to almost imperceptible "signals" from without, the poem is built up to its culmination: the Romantic contact between the poet's "soul" and the "soul" of the world:

So stillness everywhere extends her sovereign law;
All sleeps . . . save when some voice on distant darkness drifting
Sounds indistinct . . . or else some ripple laps the shore . . .
   Or when a sleepy leaf is stirring. . . .

. . . As though, concealed beneath the bark of these young trees,
Through this enchanted stillness welcome sound dispersing,
A voice, a soul unseen were reaching out to me,
And with this soul of mine conversing. . . .

                                                          (I, 264)

The "state of soul" of which we have been speaking, and which is
so personally Zhukovsky's, is invariably present not only in his
original poetry but also in his translations. This is the secret of their
capacity to endure as works of art in their own right. A striking
instance of this ability is the manner in which Zhukovsky reor-
ganizes the system of images in Goethe's "Der Fischer" (translated
as "Rybak"). Here, quite independently of the original, Zhukovsky
creates a complex image of "stillness." Once again, this is both a real
stillness and a stillness of the soul. Zhukovsky introduces an original
image: "the soul is full of cool stillness." There is nothing of this kind
in Goethe's original. His fisherman "saw calmly to his rod and line,
cool to the depths of his heart." In the same way, as we have already
shown, Zhukovsky introduced his beloved image of "stillness" into
the poem "To the Moon."

Zhukovsky was a great master of imagery. Sometimes these
images are formed not so much by the words themselves as by mood
and syntax. A characteristic example is the poem "Desire":

           Valley, melt your mists in fire!
           Scatter, gloom, and get ye gone!
           Where's the land of heart's desire?
           Where shall my soul rise again?

           There the stillness keeps her cloister,
           There the lyres have well-tuned strings,
           There from whence the gentle zephyrs
           Waft me sweet scents of the spring.

           There the golden fruits hang glistening
           From the spreading, leafy bough;
           Spiteful blizzards come not whistling
           Over grassy hill and howe. . . .

                                                          (I, 107–8)

Our first response to these verses is an awareness of their beat and rhythmic structure, the symmetry of identical syntactic forms, as exhibited in the repeated imperatives "Receive," "Scatter"; the repeated question "where?"; and the fourfold answer: "There. . . ." Thanks to the emphatic imperatives and the strong rhythm, the "desire" appears rather as an incantation, the invocation of a miracle.

In the original of this poem (Schiller's "Sehnsucht"—literally "longing"), the tonal and syntactic system are quite different; they are more passively descriptive.

> Ach, aus dieses Thales Gründen,
> Die der kalte Nebel drückt,
> Könnt' ich doch den Ausgang finden,
> Ach, wie fühlt' ich mich beglückt.[13]

Although the theme of miracle is present in the original—"Only miracle might bear you to the lovely wonderland"—its linguistic imagery, the sense of expectation and invocation, are entirely Zhukovsky's creation. Through the "incantational" rhythm the metaphors come alive: we feel the misty valley must be filled with light and the thick darkness must scatter and disperse—not just figuratively, but in the literal sense of the word.

Another example closely akin to this is to be found in Zhukovsky's translation of Goethe's ballad "Mignon" (Zhukovsky calls her "Mina"). In this translation, textually quite close to the original, two changes have been introduced. In the first place, instead of the descriptively real "die Citronen blühn" ("the lemons bloom"), Zhukovsky has "the golden lemon glows amid the darkness of the trees." In the second place, the interrogative and descriptive tone is replaced by an exclamatory note (the only use of the exclamatory form by Goethe is in the refrain "Dahin! Dahin!"). In Zhukovsky's version, instead of the opening "Know'st thou the land?" we have "I know the land!" And so on right through to the end: "There a fair house stands!" "There is a mountain!" "The rock falls!" This exclamatory note pervades the whole poem, creating an impression of prophetic ecstasy, and again, as it were, suggesting "wonders." Because of this "prophetic" tone we perceive, here as well, the poet's animation of the direct, literal meaning of the word. In the line "The golden lemon glows amid the darkness of the trees" "golden" is not simply a conventional, decorative epithet, a substitute for "yellow," but a symbol of the wonderful. Added animation is achieved by the metaphor "burns"; this truly "golden" lemon seems indeed to burn in an enchanted forest.

In the finale, the exclamatory mood to which we have become accustomed is suddenly replaced by the interrogative: "But shall I ever be there?"; and this shift, as much as the actual question, emphasizes still more the unattainability of this legendary land. Without diluting in any way the formal accuracy of his translation, Zhukovsky has wrought a fundamental change of image. Simply by altering the tone he has transformed Goethe's image of a beautiful but real country into that of a kind of fairyland.

Both in his translations and in his original poetry, Zhukovsky achieves profound effects of meaning through his skill in discovering ever new combinations of words, mood, and rhythm. In the poem "Sentiment of Spring," it is again mood that plays the chief part. In eight verses out of twelve, questions are addressed to abstract and inanimate objects. The singsong smoothness of the rhythm gives lyrical feeling to this interrogative mood while at the same time the direct form of address to the wind, the torrent, and the spring "animate" them. Adjectives and adverbs such as "light," "sweetly," "softly," "enchanted" lend this animation a romantic significance. The torrent "plays," the clouds "fly," the "migrant spring" returns; amid the common life of nature the soul of man reawakens too. A pantheistic feeling for the world is conveyed by the poet's material, sensual image of this life of nature.

CHAPTER 3

The Lyric and History

I *The Type of Zhukovsky's Elegy*

ZHUKOVSKY'S lyric poetry addresses itself to very deep layers of human consciousness, deeper than those reached by his fellow reformer of poetry, Konstantin Batyushkov. These two men created Russian classic lyric poetry of the nineteenth century; Pushkin drew support from them both. As poetic phenomena, Zhukovsky and Batyushkov are closely akin; and yet, at the same time, they are almost polar opposites. They are akin insofar as both shaped intimate lyric poetry into a medium conveying general concepts of life, and to the extent that both conceived of the "inner" life of men, not as a small part of a greater world, but as the criterion by which the values of that world were to be judged. They are also related in that both attempted to create a high, firmly ideal, peculiarly poetic world, in which general, human, moral (Zhukovsky) and aesthetic (Batyushkov) values find their sublimation. Batyushkov's ideal, however, is oriented toward the life of this earth. A melancholy strain and, in his later poetry, a note of profound tragedy are characteristics of this poet; they spring from the poet's increasing awareness of the impossibility of attaining to any ideal in view of the mutability of everything lovely upon this earth. Zhukovsky's ideal does not share this tragic quality of unattainability, for it is understood from the beginning as an eternal "treasure in heaven," in the New Testament sense.

With his elegant epicureanism, Batyushkov was passionately oriented toward antiquity, which he saw as a world of harmonious humanity. From this derived Batyushkov's "Neoclassicism," which is closely related to the Classicism of Winckelmann, Goethe, and Hölderlin and, at the same time, has much in common with the tradition of French hedonistic and erotic verse. Zhukovsky's

67

background is the German and English Preromantic tradition; thematically, Zhukovsky's poetry draws upon the Christian Middle Ages.

Batyushkov conveys the feelings of his lyrical hero more expressively and with more differentiation than does Zhukovsky; similarly, Batyushkov placed greater emphasis on elaborating principles of "personal" romanticism. Professor Viktor Vinogradov correctly demonstrates how Pushkin founded the elaboration of his Romantic style largely on his poetic apprenticeship to Batyushkov.[1] Batyushkov's poetry came closer to depicting the actual *process of the life of the soul*, though in summary terms.

The summary manner and the conventional manner are different stylistic categories. The summary style leaves the realm of life "behind the lines," as it were; yet, while it actually shows life but little, it assumes its presence in proportions and forms that are wholly real for contemporary man. The conventional style, on the contrary, makes extensive use of material detail, revels in "empirical" description (the everyday life and feelings of Batyushkov's lyrical hero) but sees all these essentially as signs, symbols, the elaboration of genuine reality in images, a style which, to a great extent, goes back to bookish cultural traditions.

From the very beginning, Zhukovsky created an elegy of a quite different type from Batyushkov's. In Batyushkov's work the dominating principle was the demonstration of feelings by revealing their external, physical manifestations, as in the following lines:

> To steal a glance toward her bridegroom courage fails,
> Her clear eyes are cast down, now flushed is she, now pale,
> Most like the moon in clouds.[2]

The expressive quality of these outward manifestations of feeling has earned Batyushkov's poetry the epithet "plastic," in the sense of visual, sculptural.

Zhukovsky, on the other hand, concentrates entirely on the actual course of emotions. Not their outward signs and manifestations, but the inner state of the soul is invariably the object of his art. The principle of Zhukovsky's poetry—to convey emotions "from within"—had a decisive influence on the development of Russian lyric poetry as a whole. It could even be said that Zhukovsky works in accordance with a method that is supremely and specifically lyrical. Everywhere, however, his extreme "nonindividuality" can be perceived. As a rule, Zhukovsky avoids the "egocentric" lyric forms: the use of the pronoun "I," accentuated by rhythm and mood in phrases grouped toward the center of the verse, is *not* a characteristic of his poetry. It is possible to cite many examples of his use of the pronoun "I" in such a way as to transfer the emphasis to other words in the same line, for example: "I thought you immortal" (*"ia tebia* bessmertnym pochital"); "With what a merry heart I'll meet my turn to die" ("S kakim *veseliem* ya budu umirat' ") ("On the Death of Andrey Turgenev"); and so on.

In the elegy "Evening," famous for its lyricism, the first person singular "I" is to be met with only once! In many poems it is overshadowed by the "you" that personifies the person to whom a given poem is addressed: "I love you—I live in you"; "Where is the name for *you*? . . . There is no lyre for *you*. . . ." There is no reason to doubt that this treatment of the pronoun was a quite deliberate literary technique. By contrast, Batyushkov wrote to Gnedich in 1811:

I discover them, my friend . . . *I*-Tibullus, and that's the truth. . . . That is all *my* confession. *I* am not in love.

> *I* swore never to love again
> . . . .
>
> And *I*—am somewhat of a coward!
> *I* am in love with myself.

I have become or want to become a complete I-man. . . .[3]

Yet another word was invariably accentuated in Zhukovsky's poetry: "soul." "Ah, thither, thither would my *soul* have flown"; "It dissolved my very *soul*/ In its balmy stillness"; "O, little star, o *soul* of mine"; among others.

In "The Flower of the Convenant," the word "soul" occurs eight times, and each time it is strongly accentuated. At the end of the poem it is presented purposely as the focal point of a bold image.

> The soul's ambassador, heard by the soul,
> faithful flower, your wordless converse holds
> So much that in our words may not be told.

(I, 325)

In Zhukovsky's poetry the concept of the soul is central. For him, "the soul" is not individual. It is, rather, that which people hold in common as a gift, that is, a uniting rather than a dividing factor.

In the elegy "On the Death of Her Majesty the Queen of Württemberg," the poet depicts the death of Ekaterina Pavlovna, the sister of Alexander I, not as the death of a queen (the word itself figures only in the title), but as the death of a young and beautiful woman, a happy wife and mother. The poem shows us the tragic experience of a family suddenly deprived of wife and mother. Here too, Zhukovsky remains faithful to his nonsocial principle of portraying people, and here too, we perceive the opposite pole, as it were, of his suprasocial humanism. At one pole is the "villager," at the other, the king and queen, and everywhere Zhukovsky sees only that which is important to him—"the soul" of man:

> Poor widowed husband, say, oh say,
> Why keep this stubborn vigil over her?
> The welcome from her face has fled away,
> And in her eyes no recognition stirs . . .
> . . . .
>
> Bridegroom, they call! Cast from your widowed brow
> The bridal crown! And on the last long road,
> Poor father, lead your orphaned children now
> To see their mother to her last abode.
>
> (I, 318–19)

In this elegy, Zhukovsky suggests with great power both the human experience of loss and the idea of human thought thrown into confusion by the cruelty of fate.

Zhukovsky's new understanding of the life of the soul was a great contribution. It was not that he set greater store by individual experience as such, or that he invested the personal with general significance, considering it important as a matter of principle. Fundamentally, in fact, it was precisely the reverse. He so expanded the boundaries of man's inner life that they became inherently capable of encompassing matters that were even beyond Batyushkov's scope. In his understanding of the life of the soul, Zhukovsky brought about a genuine revolution which was not, however, fully understood or appreciated at the time.

We have seen how great a role the so-called external world plays in Zhukovsky's poetry. This is simultaneously the sphere of goodness, morality, truth, and religion; the mysterious realm of "wonder"; and the sphere of civic duty, citizenship, and patriotism.

Zhukovsky's most important achievement is his power to make people respond to "general" concepts as to a part of their own personal, inward, spiritual life. "All the world was crammed into my heart," he exclaims in "Dreams" ("Mechty"), and in that Romantic formula we have the impulse for all later Russian lyric poetry: it retains its significance to this day.

There had occurred a mutual enrichment of the individual (the poet's "own") and the general. The general had ceased to be "external." A new and broader comprehension of the spiritual world was also expressed by Zhukovsky's favorite concept of the soul. This concept expresses the complex *wholeness* of human nature.

Zhukovsky's widening of the sphere of emotions and the inclusion of values that had theretofore been looked upon as belonging rather to the sphere of "reason" proved a great enrichment of lyric poetry, enabling it to compete more adequately with other art forms in the portrayal of the essence of the spiritual life.

Some of Zhukovsky's more remarkable works are in the field of the "poetry of thought," efforts to give form to a complex attempt to understand the laws governing human life. This objective often leads the poet into the realms of tragedy and philosophy. These trends are most vividly expressed in the "antique" ballads; in the poem "The Flower of the Covenant," in the letter to Aleksandra Fyodorovna (1818); and, most particularly, in the elegy "On the Death of Her Majesty the Queen of Württemberg."

In this elegy, human thought itself is shown as a function of the "soul"—Zhukovsky does not separate thought from feeling. This tendency had also been characteristic of the Sentimental meditative elegy, although there "sensibility" had been, as it were, an emotional counterpoint to perfectly rational thought. Here, the combination of "thought" and "feeling" was rather mechanical.

In Zhukovsky's poetry, thought and "state of soul," sententious statement and feeling, didactic utterance and Romantic dualism, are combined in a single complex. Intense thought seeks the meaning behind human life and human feelings:

O, visitor from heaven, you are flown;
You stayed on earth for all too brief a space;
We dreamed that we might claim you as *our own*
And that your home was with us in *this* place. . . .
But Fate, the fierce destroyer, struck you down
And—suddenly—of you there was no trace.
The beautiful had withered in full flower. . . .
No beauty here can bloom beyond the hour!

Misfortune waits for all, unheard, unseen,
And ambush threatens us on every way.
No shelter for our heads: where't has not been
It will be, and indifferently will slay.
And from this mortal life there is no screen;
Naught will the inescapable allay.
All walk under the menace of the One;
All here shall say of joy: over and done.

(I, 315)

Here, the dramaticism of psychological detail is combined with solemn pathos and philosophical generalization. This is the poet's *credo*. The importance of nouns and words of "general" meaning, full of universally applicable significance, contradicts the common and rather shallow criticism that Zhukovsky's poetic lexicon is dominated by vague, impressionistic adjectives. In this poem, the words "life," "grief," "joy," and "past" all carry a weight of philosophical significance that derives from the traditions of eighteenth-century poetry. Even the adjectives here are generalized through being made nouns: "The beautiful has withered in full flower. . . ./ No beauty here can bloom beyond the hour" (the translator here has succumbed to the understandable temptation to substitute an abstract noun in the second line, but Zhukovsky uses the adjectival form twice: "Prekrasnoe pogiblo v pyshnom tsvete. . . . / Takov udel prekrasnogo na svete!").

Zhukovsky is the author of the aphorism "To be happy is to think."[4] Thought become experience—that is the essence of Zhukovsky's lyric poetry.

II   *Zhukovsky's Relation to the Decembrists and Pushkin*

"No one has or will have a style to equal his in power and variety"—this remark made by Pushkin about Zhukovsky, is not, of course, to be taken literally for the whole history of Russian poetry.

The comment on the "variety" of Zhukovsky's style specifically recognized his enlargement of "the life of the soul" and the inclusion therein of values which, in the eighteenth century, had been considered attributes of pure reason. Zhukovsky did not only attribute a higher significance to the inner world as such, but he gave a deeply personal sense to things which, in poetry of the old style, had seemed "external" and "general." This was a development of decisive significance for later Russian lyric poetry. As Belinsky penetratingly remarked, "Zhukovsky's service to art as a whole really consisted in the fact that he made Russian poetry capable of expressing content."[5]

After Zhukovsky wrote, everything in lyric poetry was drawn into the sphere of personal experience: not just love, friendship, and so on, but also politics, religion, philosophy, and even art itself. This new principle was first adapted by the Decembrist poets, who came to condemn Zhukovsky only after 1824. With the exception of Pavel Katenin's group, none of them avoided the elegiac theme, but rather followed Zhukovsky's lead in attempting to blend it with the "civic." And only after 1824, when their poetry began to serve the immediate aim of stirring the reader to rebellion, did this trend begin to decline among them, only to revive with greater power in their own poetry after the unsuccessful rising of 1825, and in Lermontov's poetry.

At the beginning of the 1820s Vilgelm Kyukhelbeker was a prolific pioneer of the "civic elegy." An example of this genre is his "Nice" ("Nitstsa," 1821). Not all the verses of this poem are of equal merit. However, the poet does succeed in the most important respect: he shows human consciousness, not just as the world of "reason," but also as the world of "the soul," where the universal becomes the property of the individual, where civic sorrow is a powerful personal experience.

One of the best Decembrist poets, Kondraty Ryleev, began by keeping the civic and elegiac themes distinct from each other, making no attempt to mingle the two. He was later than Kyukhelbeker in introducing the "civic" elegy into his poetry, and it was not until about 1824 that such verses as his "Stanzas" ("Stansy"), dedicated to Aleksandr Bestuzhev, began to appear. Ryleev, however, was also obviously evolving in this direction.

Ryleev's line from the dedication of the poem "Voynarovsky": "I am not a poet but a citizen," is well known. Indeed, it brings the

poem to such an effective conclusion that we tend to forget that the
whole of the text which precedes it, some twenty lines, is scarcely to
be distinguished from any other traditional, elegiac letter in verse.

Making use of the convention of elegiac "disillusionment," Ryleev
relates how he overcame his disappointment in the life of society by
finding a twin "soul." Another poem, the "Stanzas," shows Ryleev's
disappointment with the attitude of the more cautious and moderate
Decembrists. This purely "political" disappointment is expressed in
the conventional elegiac manner:

> Soon, too soon, experience sends
> Thunderlight to scatter shade;
> Soon, too soon, my only friend,
> Have I seen how men are made.
> All men, from men indifferent turning,
> But for their own profit can
> Sham an ardent spirit, burning
> For the common good of man. . . .[6]

This poem has six stanzas; with the exception of the two quoted here,
they are all elegiac in character. In search of means to express
psychological content, Ryleev here uses the tone and rhythm of
Zhukovsky's poem "Cold Light Takes Our Joys from Us" ("Otymaet
nashi radosti"). In this 1825 letter in verse, "To Bestuzhev," he
insists upon the relationship of civic conviction and "the soul":

> The seething courage of high thought
> My soul will keep until the end;
> In young men's hearts 'tis not for naught
> Love burns for public good, my friend. . . .[7]

One of the most powerful feelings in Ryleev's poetry is the love of
freedom; the most important quality of his soul is his civic interests.
Ryleev writes his real "love poems," not about love of woman but
about love of country, as in the poem "No, I Do Not Desire Your
Love" ("Ia ne khochu liubvi tvoei," 1824). This is a typical "civic
elegy," a new genre, but one which still clearly derived from the
elegy of Zhukovsky.

In 1825, Pushkin wrote to Ryleev about Zhukovsky, using an
image from Dante's *Divine Comedy:* "Why should we bite the

breasts of our wet-nurse? Just because our milk teeth have come through?"[8]

There is every reason to suppose that Ryleev, if his career had not been so tragically interrupted, would have become a direct precursor of Lermontov. His poem "The Citizen" ("Grazhdanin") already has a Lermontovian ring to it. It is a very personal poem, but at the same time its civic pathos is remarkably intense.

What we have just said about Decembrist poetry also applies directly to Pushkin. In his "Letter to Chaadaev" ("Poslanie k Chadaevu"), in "The Country" ("Derevnia"), and in a number of other verses, Pushkin's love of his country and love of freedom are presented as the emotions of an individual human heart.

> But still desire in us burns high;
> Although by fateful power oppressed
> Our ready spirits know no rest
> And heed our country's rallying-cry.
>
> (Pushkin, II, 72)

In the "Prisoner of the Caucasus" and Pushkin's poetry of the southern period, lyrical motifs are interwoven with the theme of freedom, the "elegiac" with the civic. The prisoner's love of freedom is presented, not so much as a moral conviction, as an attribute of his "soul":

> Ah, Freedom! It was Thee alone
> He sought throughout this desert world.
> Grown cold to dreams and poetry
> By passions sentiment he curbed,
> Yet heard all songs inspired by Thee
> With deep emotion. . . .
>
> (Pushkin, IV, 95)

Thus Pushkin managed to convey the "Byronic" view of man proper to the early 1820s through the same elegiac style first elaborated by Zhukovsky.

One of Zhukovsky's favorite themes was that of creative work, of inspiration, revealed through its inner significance as a manifestation of "the life of the soul."

Pushkin's understanding of poetry was immeasurably broader than Zhukovsky's, and included, among other elements, the active

civic sentiment inherent in his character. As a poet Pushkin was a
tribune of the people, and a prophet. But he was more than that.
The image is more comprehensive:

> And I forget the world—and in sweet stillness I
> Am sweetly lulled to sleep by my free fancy. . . .

("Autumn," III, 321)

These verses are at one and the same time immensely far from
Zhukovsky, yet, in much that is of importance, also dependent on
him. Zhukovsky had prepared the ground for the basic view of
inspiration as a "state of soul," as a lofty spiritual need and pleasure.
And "sweet stillness" was an image originally created by Zhukovsky.

It was Zhukovsky who introduced "inspiration" into poetry as a
"verbal theme" of the first importance. Pushkin was extremely
attached to this word, which Zhukovsky was the first to invest with a
new psychological meaning:

> Again you're here, most gracious Visitation,
> My Genius, aerial friend of long ago;
> Again on waves of old hallucinations
> Familiar Dream, my soul you overflow.
> Come then, o friend! Waft back the inspiration
> Of youth, and past delights about me blow. . . .
>> (From the introduction to the ballad
>> "The Twelve Sleeping Maidens." II, 84)

These last verses have a purely Pushkinian ring to them. Indeed, a
direct parallel to them may be found in Pushkin's own poetry:
"Come then, and by the flame of magic story—Make live again the
legends of the heart . . ." ("The 19th of October," 1825).

Also important to Pushkin was the fact that Zhukovsky did not
separate art and inspiration from other aspects of the life of the soul,
or from other lyric themes (love, friendship, memory). The following lines from the poem "To V. A. Perovsky" in their affinity with
the lyrical digressions of *Evgeny Onegin* may serve as an example of
Zhukovsky's "Pushkinian" style:

> Love flashed upon my sight again
> And with a soul renewed, aflame,

> In haste I seized my lyre—and
> A ripple of familiar sound
> Awoke beneath my eager hand!
> Then in the dead new life I found,
> And looked—a poet, as of old—
> About me on a world unsouled. . . .

(I, 330)

Here we have the principle of the oneness of man's inner world so dear to Pushkin, the mutual interconnection and influence of art, thought, and love. In chapter 8 of *Onegin*, we find Pushkin echoing the verbal image of the poet created by Zhukovsky.

The lyrical subject of the verses we have quoted is close to that of Pushkin's "I Mind Me of the Wondrous Moment," where the dead comes to life again and the poetic attitude to the world is also reawakened. There are also actual line-by-line echoes, as in Zhukovsky's "Love flashed *upon my sight* again" and Pushkin's "When first you broke *upon my sight*"; in Zhukovsky's "with a *soul renewed*," and Pushkin's "The day came for the soul to quicken"; among others.

In passages where he is writing within a certain pattern of images, Pushkin makes generous use of Zhukovsky's phraseology. We have seen that the expression "spirit of pure beauty" in Pushkin's "I Mind Me of the Wondrous Moment" was, originally, used by Zhukovsky. Of course, the important thing is not the phrase itself but the ideal expressed in it; and here there was no gulf between Pushkin and Zhukovsky:

> I mind me of the wondrous moment
> When first you broke upon my sight,
> A vision of a fleeting moment,
> A spirit of pure beauty bright.
>
> The day came for my soul to quicken:
> Again you broke upon my sight
> A fleeting momentary vision,
> A spirit of pure beauty bright.
>
> The heart beats high in exaltation,
> And, reawakened, does perceive
> Divinity and inspiration,
> Abundant life, and tears, and love.

(Pushkin, II, 406–7)

In Zhukovsky's poem "My Youthful Muse, in Times Gone By" the subject is also the poet's path in life, the temporary loss of inspiration and hope which had been given him by the "spirit of pure beauty" as an incarnation of love and poetry. In subject, tone, and rhythm these verses of Zhukovsky's are the direct predecessors of Pushkin's poem:

> The flowers of dreaming melancholy
> And life's fair flowers of best delight
> I lay upon your altar holy,
> O spirit of pure beauty bright!
>
> For while her splendor's not yet sped
> Beyond the soul's reach to attain:
> The old enchantment is not dead!
> And what has been will be again.
>
> (I, 367–68)

Pushkin's "I Mind Me of the Wondrous Moment" not only bears vivid witness to his deep indebtedness to Zhukovsky, but also illustrates the distance which divided them. Pushkin's poem reads like a dramatic account from "real life." Zhukovsky, who was also writing about earthly love, creates an apparently symbolic image.

One theme of Zhukovsky's poetry particularly sympathetic to Pushkin was that of *writing as work*, a labor which, for the poet, is nonetheless a joy in itself and its own reward.

This conception is closely linked to the idea of true and false judgment. For both Zhukovsky and Pushkin, the poet is his own supreme judge. Hence derive the phraseological correspondences between Pushkin's brilliant poems and certain lines from his predecessor's poetry. The same theme and the same mood are found in Pushkin's aphorism "But you, you remain firm . . ." from the poem "To the Poet" ("Poetu"), and in Zhukovsky's "Write, and be firm . . ." from his "Letter to Prince Vyazemsky and V. L. Pushkin" ("K kn. Vyazemskomu i V. L. Pushkinu").

In Pushkin's poetry, images from Zhukovsky and, in fact, from other poets who may be regarded as his forerunners, are often present in the form of "raw material" that has undergone a process of radical readaptation. What in Zhukovsky's poetry was, as it were, the artistic "goal," the basic "object," is, in Pushkin, nothing but a means, a component part of a quite different whole. The image from

Zhukovsky has become a detail of a new structure, grandiose not so much in its external proportions as in the complexity and wealth of its historical and literary associations.

III *Zhukovsky and the Development of Modern Russian Lyric Poetry*

Perhaps the cardinal problem of Zhukovsky's age was the relationship between the "public" life of humanity and the individual, spiritual life of each human being as a separate entity. For all their understanding of the complexity and tragedy of the human condition, and for all their differences of character, Batyushkov, Zhukovsky, and Pushkin shared essentially the same attitude toward this problem, which might be called a "harmonizing" attitude. It was manifested in stylistic harmony and in a certain deliberate "poetization" of things. As a result, the poets faced the necessity of making a highly selective use of words. After all, not all words in any language can be made "poetic." By comparison with Zhukovsky and Batyushkov, Pushkin made an immense contribution toward expanding the vocabulary of Russian poetry. Even he, however, avoided words that he considered "expressed things in a vulgar way," as, for instance, *nalizat'sia* instead of *napit'sia p'ianym* (roughly equivalent to "to get sozzled" instead of "to get drunk").[9] Pushkin was in fact one of the last advocates of the "poeticization" of life. For this reason, among others, Zhukovsky's poetry remained close to Pushkin's "spirit" at all stages of its development (let us remember Pushkin's words, already quoted, concerning Zhukovsky's beneficent influence "on the spirit of our literature").

In extending the vocabulary of poetry beyond the rather narrow bounds set by Batyushkov and Zhukovsky, Pushkin showed a veritable genius for poeticizing "everyday," sometimes even coarse words, as in *Onegin*:

> The herd
> Drives not the cattle from the byre. . . .
> . . . The maiden by the cottage fire
> Spins neath a crackling faggot's light,
> Companion of her winters' nights.
>
> (Pushkin, VI, 90)

Here everything conceivable has been done to alter the lexical coloring of the word "byre" (*khlev*), so it really does not occur to the reader that the word is "coarse." To begin with, it is used in close proximity to the word *deva* ("maiden"). *Khleva* and *deva* not only rhyme, but *deva* is also given a place of particular emphasis in the verse as a whole, thanks to the pause necessitated by the enjambment "*deva—priadet* . . ." (literally "the maiden—spins"). The lofty word "maiden" is, incidentally, used to describe a peasant lass (*devka* was the word used for such a person by a critic of Pushkin's time), and her humble "faggot" (*luchinka*) is dignified by the elegant, "Karamzinian" paraphrase "companion of her winters' nights." The word *khlev* is thus transformed by these other words to such an extent that it almost assumes a "poetic" coloration. Pushkin's attitude was his own. One of its sources, however, was undoubtedly Zhukovsky's lyricism. Later, the "poeticizing" principle was called into question and, in the lyric poetry of the twentieth century, the criterion of "poeticality" was pronounced totally invalid by many poets. What we have here, then, is not an eternal or constant characteristic of lyric poetry, but a peculiar feature of one specific style. The example of Pushkin demonstrates that the basic genre of the new lyric verse was the elegy, but that the elegiac style was capable of being enriched by additional infusions of color and feeling. Even harmony, such a basic attribute of the elegy, gradually yielded to other stylistic techniques. Nevertheless, there can be no doubt that the poetic "school" of Karamzin, Batyushkov, and Zhukovsky did prevail in its struggle with opposing trends. It opened the way to the expression of the most varied feelings and thoughts through lyric poetry, creating a new vessel for philosophical and social content.

In the 1820s and 1830s lyric poetry evolved toward a more profound treatment of the "intimate" genres. It became capable of embracing, understanding, and evaluating the world's unlimited variety. In Pushkin's lyric poetry the inner world of the individual becomes the prism through which there are reflected problems properly pertaining to history and sociology. For Baratynsky and Tyutchev, philosophical problems on a truly cosmic scale were to become the content of their own souls.

Indeed it may be argued that all of Russian lyric poetry, with its characteristic, "intimate" reflection of political, historical, and philosophical themes, was essentially a continuation of Zhukovsky's lyricism. Finally, it is possible to trace a direct connection between

Zhukovsky and one of the most interesting phenomena of modern Russian lyric poetry: twentieth-century symbolism.

Among Zhukovsky's younger contemporaries his genuine followers were, of course, not the mere imitators who copied the letter of his themes and style, but those who continued to progress along the path he had pioneered and in lyric poetry to expand the boundaries of man's inner world. As this process continued, the elegy was gradually transformed, a transformation noticeable both in the work of the greater and of the lesser poets who would continue Zhukovsky's work. In this respect, Vyazemsky's poetry, although entirely concentrated on reproducing the life and way of thought of the contemporary world and flowing from the common Karamzinian source, owed much to Zhukovsky. Even in his satirical pieces, where private interests were broadened to include an ever widening circle of phenomena and the general was considered as the particular, Vyazemsky always took Zhukovsky's experience into account.

The vivid, brilliant poet Nikolay Yazykov owed less to Zhukovsky than did Vyazemsky. Still, he revered Zhukovsky profoundly, and, in the poem "Undine," inspired by Zhukovsky's verse legend of the same title, he expressed a preference for the "lofty stillness" of Zhukovsky's poetry over that other poetry in which, in his words, "there is much thunder." Here Yazykov seems to be indulging in self-criticism. Yazykov and Baratynsky, who was the same age as he, represented the rising generation of elegists of the 1820s (Pushkin, although only a few years their senior, nevertheless referred to them in the early 1820s as "younger" poets). Yazykov, far from imitating Zhukovsky's elegies, used them as a kind of springboard in the sense that his own writing is conceived as a kind of spontaneous polemic with the older poet. But even this attitude is simply another form of continuity.

In his love elegies, Yazykov invariably asserts the opposite to Zhukovsky. His lyrical hero does not "dream," or "sigh," or "lament." He depicts "states of soul" quite different from those painted by Zhukovsky, but the significant fact is that he does depict them.

The tradition of the "high" elegy, with all the hallmarks of the genre, is far stronger in the works of Baratynsky, a great and profoundly original poet. His poetry is a continuation of Zhukovsky's "melancholy" elegy and, in its own way, a reply to it. In some of his verses Baratynsky follows very closely in Zhukovsky's footsteps in images, phraseology, mood.

Even in those poems—among the most powerful that he wrote—in which Baratynsky appears as Zhukovsky's opposite, as a poet of uniquely profound pessimism, the connection is not broken. It merely becomes polemical. Baratynsky presents his solutions to the problems of human life in direct opposition to the solutions offered by Zhukovsky; yet the problems themselves, the sphere of interests, are the same. Both poets penetrate the very essence of the radical problems of existence—the meaning of life, death, and the immortality of the soul. There can be no doubt that Baratynsky subjected the content and images of his teacher's lyric poetry to a serious and fundamental reworking.

In Baratynsky's famous poem "Autumn" ("Osen' "), we find textually polemical echoes of Zhukovsky's poems. Baratynsky ran his fingers, one could say, swiftly and surely over Zhukovsky's keyboard, resetting motifs and verbal expressions from the elegy "On the Death of Her Majesty the Queen of Württemberg." In "Autumn," in the image of the comfortless, symbolic "evening of the year," the very word "evening" is perhaps a signal, a polemical echo from Zhukovsky's most famous elegy, in which sadness over the passing of life had been so exquisitely muted by the radiant harmony of the verse.

Baratynsky's manner, as opposed to Zhukovsky's songlike generalized style, was deeply discriminating: no Russian poet has had such a capacity for contrast and differentiation as Baratynsky. This differentiated style is necessarily devoid of unity of poetic mood. It is rich in paradox and antonyms, thereby foreshadowing the poetry of the twentieth century.

The lofty, dreamy tone of Zhukovsky's poetry expresses his belief in the noble qualities of the human soul, in its ability to comprehend the meaning of life, though hidden from more prosaic minds.

In Baratynsky's poetry these beautiful criteria of the soul and the world are perceived as great illusions. Yet the poet by no means breaks away altogether from these criteria. His use of antonyms is also in deliberate contrast to that sweet, sonorous harmony whose classic form had been elaborated in the Russian lyrics of Zhukovsky.[10]

In the 1820s, Zhukovsky's direct successors in the narrow sense of that word (the adherents of his elegiac "school" and "melancholy"

style) were the second-rate poets Andrey Podolinsky, Pyotr Plet-
nev, Vasily Tumansky and Viktor Teplyakov,[11] as well as the rather more talented Ivan Kozlov. Another member of his literary circle was Pushkin's close friend, Anton Delvig. Delvig, however, although a great admirer of Zhukovsky, made no attempt to follow in
his footsteps. Not greatly gifted as a lyric poet, Delvig avoided the
lyric genre *per se* and excelled instead at composing elegant,
stylized idylls in the antique spirit, and romances in the Russian folk
tradition. Nevertheless, the influence of Zhukovsky's elegiac style is
to be felt even in these genres, particularly in the romances.

As for Kozlov, Zhukovsky was his teacher and model in the fullest
sense of the word. For him, Zhukovsky's poetry was not merely a
literary school, but the source of his strength and support in personal misfortune (grave bodily indisposition and blindness).

Kozlov followed Zhukovsky in his lyrical "sadness" and
"thoughtfulness," as well as in his deliberately "poeticizing" style.
He differed from Zhukovsky in the greater intensity of his plaints
and the dominance of lamentation. Kozlov's poetry is now primarily
of historical interest as the link between Zhukovsky and Lermontov.

Lermontov himself was deeply indebted to Zhukovsky. In
contradistinction to Zhukovsky, Lermontov's romantic lyric poetry
is individualistic, wholly oriented toward frank, personal confession.
Indeed, Zhukovsky was hostile to Lermontov's individualism,
bordering on "demonism," and to his melancholy, bordering on
despair. Nevertheless, much in Lermontov's poetry, as in
Baratynsky's, was merely the extension to its logical conclusion of
the melancholy disillusion of the elegy. If Baratynsky took
Zhukovsky's verse as his point of departure, moving in the general
direction of an "existentialist" world view, Lermontov moved from
the same point of departure towards Byronic spleen and *Welt-
schmerz*. Zhukovsky's experience as the first Russian lyric poet
to express man's complaints at life in the language of the elegy was
deeply assimilated by Lermontov. Indeed, it could not have been
otherwise, since, unlike other forms of literature, lyric poetry is
extremely dependent on its own national tradition.

Lermontov endows the elegiac genre with an absolute
"egocentricity," but, on the whole, he still retains the structure of
the genre—that is, if we except his lyrical "fragments." The principle of the lyrical meditation is still dominant in Lermontov, although his forms of speech are more expressive and colorful. Above

and beyond this assimilation, the younger poet also adopted the melodic tonal system so carefully elaborated by Zhukovsky, so that even the most original of Lermontov's mature poems are often constructed according to the melodic scheme of Zhukovsky's verses. An example of this is "The Branch from Palestine" ("Vetka Palestiny").

Of the following generation, Apollon Grigorev, Yakov Polonsky, Nikolay Nekrasov, and, most particularly, Afanasy Fet, adopted many motifs and stylistic features of Zhukovsky's poetry, prolonging the line of continuity from Zhukovsky to Vladimir Solovyov, the immediate forerunner of Russian Symbolism. Aleksandr Blok, Vladimir Solovyov's younger contemporary and "disciple," wrote: "My first inspiration came from Zhukovsky."[12]

CHAPTER 4

The Ballad and Russia

I *General Characterization of the Ballads*

ZHUKOVSKY's ballads are as important an element of his poetic production as his lyric poetry. They played a unique part in the development of the descriptive style of modern Russian poetry. They were also of general educational value to a wide reading public, making them familiar with the legends and histories of other lands. If Zhukovsky's lyric poetry was fully appreciated in all its profundity only by other poets, the ballads, with their dramatic subjects and engrossing fantasies, were immediately attractive to every imaginable type of reader, and enjoyed immense popularity.

Almost all of Zhukovsky's thirty-nine ballads are translations. Many are "free" translations, in which the poet recreates the sense and the story, but does not seek to follow the original text literally. In the more exact translations, the text of the original is reproduced, but even here there are differences, since an identical artistic translation from one language into another is an impossibility.

Zhukovsky has rightly been called a translator of great genius. To anticipate somewhat, we might quote here the remark of K. A. Varnhagen von Ense, a scholar of Greek and Russian, who in speaking of Zhukovsky's translation of the *Odyssey*, said: "We Germans have nothing so felicitous."[1]

Zhukovsky himself was aesthetically perfectly justified in recommending to one of his German friends who knew no Russian the following original way to gain an impression of his own work: he was to reread, in the original, twelve verses translated from Schiller; Goethe's "Erlkönig" and "Die Vergänglichkeit"; seven poems by Johann Hebel; Friedrich Rückert's *Nal und Damajanti* and *Rostem und Suharb*; and Friedrich La Motte-Fouqué's *Undine*. "When you have read all these works, believe, or try to make yourself

believe, that they have all been translated from the Russian, from
Zhukovsky, or vice versa: then you will have an idea of the best
things I have written; then you will have a full, true understanding
of my poetic talent, only very much more advantageous to me than if
you had known it *in naturalibus.*"[2]

In a specialized study of Zhukovsky's translations the high perfection of his work led a critic to write of "that virtuosity, creating
the impression of completely independent creative writing, of
improvisation, without which there cannot be the impression of
miracle."[3]

The impression of "miracle" is constructed of many component
parts. Their foundation, however, is a profound synthesis of theme,
image, and language.

Zhukovsky's translated ballads read like original works because
they are distinguished by a peculiar, poetic "emotive quality" that
conveys to the reader a sense of complete spontaneity of imagination
even in an exact rendering of another's text. This almost unattainable ideal was, in fact, achieved by Zhukovsky.

Naturally, this emotive quality and spontaneity of imagination
may only be achieved when the author of the translation enjoys a
great inner affinity with the author of the original. Hence derive the
shading and accentuation of those motifs which are particularly close
to the translator and yet which, at the same time, are not "secondary" but rather essential to the work being translated. Zhukovsky
chose for translation only such works as were fundamentally in
harmony with his own inner world.

In his best ballads, Zhukovsky preserves the most important
features of the original and even gives them added emphasis, while
slightly downgrading secondary themes and incidents not essential
to its basic concept. Thus, in Schiller's ballads, he accentuates the element of wistful longing, the eternal reaching out for the unattainably beautiful and, at the same time, he somewhat weakens, but by
no means neutralizes, the historical coloring. As one would expect
from the overall structure of his poetry, Zhukovsky's lyrical sentiment lends his ballads a certain generalized character, in the sense
that he seeks primarily to recreate essence instead of detail.
However, that does not mean in the least that Zhukovsky conveys
no details at all. If that were the case, we could not even speak of
exact translation. On the contrary, Zhukovsky frequently finds
images almost identical with those of the original.

It is possible to distinguish among Zhukovsky's ballads a group of genuine masterpieces in the art of translation. These include above all his translations from Schiller: "Die Kraniche von Ibykus," "Ritter Toggenburg," "Der Graf von Hapsburg," "Das Siegesfest," "Der Taucher," "Der Ring des Polykrates," and "Das Eleusische Fest." Also magnificent are "A Ballad Showing How an Old Woman Rode Double, and Who Rode Before Her" and "Queen Orraca and the Five Martyrs of Morocco" from Robert Southey, Walter Scott's "The Eve of St. John," Goethe's "Erlkönig" and "Der Fischer," and Ludwig Uhland's "Harald."

More extensive departures from the original have been introduced into Schiller's "Kassandra" and "Klage der Ceres," into Southey's "Donica" and "God's Judgement on a Wicked Bishop," Uhland's "Durand" (translated as "Alonzo"), "König Karls Meerfahrt," "Junker Rechberger" (translated as "Rytsar' Rollon"), and "Roland Schildträger," Walter Scott's "The Gray Brother" (translated as "Pokaianie"); François-Augustin Paradis de Moncrif's "Les Constantes amours d'Alix et d'Alexis" (translated as "Alina i Alsim"). Here, too, however, the translations are intended to be faithful renderings of the original. Certain rhythmic changes are linked to the exigencies of Russian prosody.

Free translations are from Southey's "Rudiger" (translated as "Adelstan") and "Lord William" (translated as "Barvik"); Oliver Goldsmith's "The Deserted Village" (translated as "Pustynnik"); Uhland's "Die Rache," "Drei Lieder," and "Graf Eberhards Weissdorn" (translated as "Staryi rytsar' "); David Mallet's "Edwin and Emma" (translated as "Elvina i Edvin"); and Thomas Campbell's "Lord Ullin's Daughter" (Translated as "Ullin i ego doch' "). "Lyudmila" is a free adaptation of Bürger's ballad which Zhukovsky had previously translated under the original title, "Lenora."

Finally, there are Zhukovsky's own ballads: "Svetlana," "The Aeolian Harp," "Achilles," "The Captive," and "The Twelve Sleeping Maidens." In these ballads, the author simply makes use of certain motifs from the ballads of western European poets. They are, however, basically original creations. It is interesting that the more exact translations are of the most significant originals.

In spite of their thematic differences, all of Zhukovsky's thirty-nine ballads represent a single, monolithic whole, an artistic cycle held together not merely by unity of genre, but also by an underlying unity of meaning. Zhukovsky was interested in works in which questions of human behavior and the choice between good and evil were raised with particular immediacy. His ballad cycle thus condenses subject matter scattered throughout the heritage of western European poetry.

Good and evil, sharply opposed, figure in all Zhukovsky's ballads, without exception. Their source is always the heart of man itself, and the mysterious, supernatural forces that influence it. Romantic dualism is present in them, but usually in the guise of the Satanic versus the Divine Principle. God and the Devil are programmatic personages in Zhukovsky's poetry, and the Devil never appears as a Romantic spirit of protest but always, in the true, Orthodox Christian tradition, as the spirit of evil. Although medieval religious beliefs and superstitions impressed the poet from the point of view of Romantic "exoticism," he was also deeply affected by the simplicity of this faith in the miraculous "saving" and "losing" of souls.

In only four of the ballads—"Harald," "The Fisherman," "The Elf-king" ("Der Erlkönig"), and, perhaps more debateably, "Donica"—the fantastic element is not subordinated to an aesthetic function; the "miraculous" element is here shown as irrational, an attitude typical of the European preromantic and Romantic ballad.

Zhukovsky was also deeply interested in questions of destiny, of personal responsibility and retribution. Hence his interest in Schiller's "ancient" ballads. Traditionally, these problems received a more philosophical and less "decorative" treatment in poetry dealing with ancient subjects.

It would be a reasonable assumption that Zhukovsky's moral didacticism would make his ballads less a part of the Romantic than of the Sentimentalist or even Classical tradition. However, although logical, this conclusion would be purely formal. Both in their historic function in Russian literature and in their own essence, Zhukovsky's ballads are works of the Romantic school. Furthermore, as we shall see, particularly during the early period, Zhukovsky is more "archaic" in certain details than his models, and in his basic understanding of man and of the world he is often more of a Romantic. We know that he romanticized Goethe and Schiller, emphasizing the hero's aspiration to the ideal, to the unattainably beautiful. His original ballads, too, particularly the lyrical "Aeolian Harp," are purely Romantic works.

In this connection, the most important thing to bear in mind is not so much the fantastic elements nor the frequency of medieval subjects, nor yet Zhukovsky's "dualism," but rather the conception of the life of the soul as an immensely complex sum of emotional experiences seen in relation to the visible and invisible life of the world. It is this characteristic that makes Zhukovsky's ballads and his lyric poetry so palpably the work of one and the same author.

In almost all his ballads Zhukovsky emphasizes the "poetization" of objects, a specific feature of all his work. It was noted long ago that Zhukovsky always tends to soften the "rough," "folk" elements of content and style. This trait, in fact, is advanced by A. N. Veselovsky as an argument against classifying Zhukovsky with the Romantics. But if the "folk element" was considered the particular discovery of the Romantics within the framework of the literary tradition of western Europe, in Russia the whole situation was somewhat different. The by no means romantic Russian literary tradition of the eighteenth century had long since discovered the "folk element." For this reason it is at least partially correct to say that Pavel Katenin's famous "Olga" was a backward-looking, rather than a forward-looking work. Russian Romanticism developed along the lines laid down by Zhukovsky, that is, along the lines of "poeticization" (Pushkin's "Southern" poems and the work of Lermontov). The folk element, on the contrary, became a central ingredient in the formation of Russian realism: this is the function it performs in Pushkin's work.

The atmosphere of "poeticization" in Zhukovsky's ballads is purely Romantic, as in his lyric poetry. It has nothing in common with artificial literary convention. On the contrary, it creates an impression of Romantic inspiration, bringing poet and reader alike into communion with the mysteries and exalted life of the earthly realm.

In translating his ballads, Zhukovsky often softens the brighter, more varied colors, particularly in his descriptions of medieval *realia*. However, he does this with great tact and without sacrificing historical atmosphere: on the contrary, he intensifies it by concentrating on its essence. For the Russian reader, who had no "Middle Ages" in the Western sense to look back upon, an overabundance of exotic detail might have obscured this essence.

Zhukovsky emphasizes the lyricism of his ballads. This lyrical quality, more than any other single attribute, imbued his translations with the breath of original creation.

Despite their inner unity, Zhukovsky's ballads can be systematically classified in various cycles according to three basic criteria: chronological, stylistic, and thematic, although these criteria do not invariably coincide.

From the chronological point of view, it is possible to distinguish three distinct periods: 1808–1814, 1816–1822, 1828–1832. Between these periods are intervals when Zhukovsky wrote no ballads, and each period has its own type of translation.

Only in the first and second periods do we meet with original ballads; it is also characteristic of the general course of Zhukovsky's development that the majority of free adaptations belong to the first period, after which the percentage of exact translations increases until, in the last period (1828–1832), exact translations are in a majority.

The first period (1808–1814) was the most spontaneously lyrical. This is not to say that there is not a great deal of lyricism in his other ballads belonging to chronologically different categories, but only that it manifests itself in more complex forms. His "epic" qualities, the gifts of masterly description and objective narrative, developed considerably between 1816 and 1832. The moral, didactic element is present throughout.

Thematically, Zhukovsky's ballads can be divided into three groups: the national-historic (Russian), the medieval, and the ancient. The national-historic themes are concentrated in the first period—only the "Russian" ballad of the "Twelve Sleeping Maidens" was completed during the second period, in 1817. The second period is wholly devoted to subjects from the western European Middle Ages, and it is these subjects that remain numerically predominant in the third period. Subjects from the ancient world figure only at the beginning and at the end of Zhukovsky's work on the ballad. The moral and philosophical importance of the theme of antiquity was evident from the beginning but was elaborated in the later masterpieces at a deeper level.

In this study we shall treat Zhukovsky's ballads according to thematic groups, pointing out those differences in thought, style, and approach to subject matter that occur in the various chronological periods.

II *Ballads on Russian Historical Themes*

The first Russian ballad is the delightful "Lyudmila" (1808). The freest of all Zhukovsky's adaptations (although he retained the subject and general sense of Bürger's "Lenore"), the poet himself called it an "imitation."

Bürger's "Lenore," based on old German folktales of a dead bridegroom, was a typical preromantic ballad. It was excellently suited to serve as a first model from the creation of the Russian literary ballad. The line of development from "Lyudmila" to the "Eleusinian Feast" reproduces, as it were, the general course of evolution of the genre as a whole from the "naive" to the "intellectual" type of ballad.

Zhukovsky set himself the task of creating a Russian ballad on a western European model. To lend the story a national flavor, he replaces the War of 1741–1748 between Prussia and Austria, which provides the historical setting for Bürger's tale, with the Livonian wars of the sixteenth and seventeenth centuries. For the same reason, he uses words from the vocabulary of pre-Petrine Russia: *rat'* ("host" or "army"), *druzhina* ("prince's bodyguard"), and so on. He gives his heroine a Slavonic name, Lyudmila.

On the other hand, the "folk element," in the sense of a popular conception of the past of one's own country, is completely lacking in this work. Unlike Bürger, Zhukovsky makes no attempt to stylize his verse in the spirit of the "folk ballad." In fact, he could not have done so, since, in the Russian folk tradition, there is no equivalent of the kind of ballad he was attempting to reproduce, a fact which Zhukovsky's "rival," Katenin, contrived to ignore.

It was not weakness, but a perfectly correct aesthetic instinct which induced Zhukovsky to base his orientation upon the literary tradition of lyrical songs in the spirit of the folksong. The songs of such writers as Nikolay Lvov and Yury Neledinsky-Meletsky were not false, despite their artificiality, for they preserved certain genuine features of the folk genre. In his "Lyudmila," Zhukovsky does not subordinate his creativity to this tradition but makes free use of it in order to recreate the olden days of his native land. In so doing, the poet actually made the songs themselves, which before his "Lyudmila" had been accepted as a perfectly contemporary, lyrical genre, seem suddenly outdated and thereby relegated them to the realm of an irrecoverable past.

If the traditions of Russian folklore are not developed in any detail in "Lyudmila," they are nevertheless used selectively and with great skill to create a "national" style. Zhukovsky spoke to his readers in a language that combined naive sentimentality with elegant simplicity, and patriarchal, archaic dignity with subtly mellifluous sound. The achievement of this "alloy" was one of the most specific objectives of the "Russian" style of the time, and Zhukovsky could not have chosen a more suitable vehicle for a national ballad.

In this regard, we should also remember that Bürger's fantasy was by its nature foreign to the Russian folk tradition, and that the subject (a "wedding" with a dead man) is not typical of Russian folklore.

It is worth noting that in "Svetlana," where the poet is making a deliberate attempt to bring his poetry closer to the folk tradition, he introduces a basic change in the story of the ballad, breaking away from the German original: "Svetlana" centers around the subject of dreams and fortune-telling, both of which are, in fact, specifically characteristic elements of Russian folklore. In "Lyudmila," the outstanding features of Zhukovsky's poetry—lyricism and poeticization—are very much in evidence. The love lyrics set within the framework of didactic "horrors" are not without significance for the general sense of the ballad. Zhukovsky departs from his original in his conception of the character of his heroine, whom he transforms from a hardy, rather stern peasant girl into a tender, gentle maiden. Her outpourings of love and her bitter sorrow for the bridegroom she has lost in the wars are extremely affecting. In Zhukovsky's ballad, Lyudmila's despair and fidelity are so ennobled that the moralistic "retribution" to which she is subjected appears unjust (God, having heard the poor girl calling down imprecations upon this life, unites her with her beloved in the grave). In "Lyudmila" (to a higher degree than in Bürger's "Lenore") we find the impulse which leads to the idealized interpretation of virtually the same subject in the ballad "Svetlana."

Zhukovsky's efforts to give poetic form to a national Russian theme met with their greatest success in "Svetlana," over which the poet worked from 1808 to 1812. This version is the most successful of his three adaptations of "Lenore," and the furthest removed in subject. The ballad describes Russian girls engaged in the traditional rites of fortune-telling on the Eve of Epiphany. One of them expects the return of her betrothed and tells her friends of her anxiety for him. She is persuaded to take part in the rites. The timid "sweet Svetlana" sees her beloved in a mirror; he calls upon her to follow him; the lovers gallop across the snowy midnight fields in a sleigh, passing churches and peasant huts. The tender, caressing inflections of the opening lines shift to a troubled rhythm. In one of the huts Svetlana is left alone with a corpse that struggles to rise from its coffin and seize her; the corpse is Svetlana's betrothed. The girl is defended by a white dove. With a cry of horror, Svetlana awakens. But this is not the end; Zhukovsky keeps us in suspense as his heroine puzzles over the dream which seems to bode such evil for her. Again she is sad and silent—but the sound of harness bells rings out, a sleigh comes galloping up to the gate, and there before her is her beloved fiancé—alive.

As we have already said, there is no tradition involving this type of ballad in Russian folklore. Unlike Bürger, Zhukovsky set out to create a consciously literary genre. He is not so much imitating the specific folklore character of any particular instance as he is seeking to create the "general type" of this character and to synthesize its distinguishing features. As a result, "Svetlana" served as a signpost pointing out one of the paths taken by future poets in elaborating the Russian folk theme.

Zhukovsky's approach to the popular mind is, of course, different from Pushkin's. He constantly sublimates the folk element. "Svetlana" was written at a time when Russian Sentimentalism was at its height, and it contains a great many sentimental elements.

The distinguishing features of Russian national *couleur locale* were brought together in Zhukovsky's work. He was the first to offer a sort of anthology of these features, stylized, perhaps, but nevertheless expressive: winter, snow, horesedrawn sleighs with their bright harness and jingling bells (the famous image of the *troika*, though here as yet unnamed); fortune-telling, icons, peasant huts; then snow again, the winter road, the bells, the sleigh, and a hint at a "Russian wedding."

"Svetlana," for all the apparent simplicity of its main subject, is in fact artistically very complex. Thus, the heroine is not introduced into the tale immediately or directly, but only after Zhukovsky, in the first stanza, has created a "model," folklore world for her. Moreover, the description of this model world is no less important than the description of Svetlana herself. Indeed, as an inhabitant of this world apart the heroine is not so much an object of dramatic compassion, as is usually the case with the *personae* of the ballad, as she is a subject of aesthetic delight. She is brought into the story as the centerpiece of a colorful potpourri of popular superstitions, customs, and ritual songs.

> Once upon a Twelfth-Night Eve
> Maidens were soothsaying,
> Trying out old quaint beliefs;

At the gates delaying
To cast a slipper from their toes,
   To listen at the shutter,
And furrow the smooth snow with hoes.
   They brought the hens aflutter
To peck up counted grains. Then green
Earrings laid in water clean,
   Then a golden ring;
Dripped hot wax above the bowl,
And voices joined, with heart and soul
   Old sorcerous songs to sing.

(II, 18)

Against this background, Zhukovsky undoubtedly wished to portray his heroine as a characteristic type of national Russian girl, in whom the qualities he highlights are, above all, gentleness, fidelity, and resignation; this, and a reflected gleam of pure poetry from the depths of his folklore sources. Nowadays, Zhukovsky's heroine may seem too much of a poetic convention, too idealized, particularly because of the—to the modern palate— overly generous dash of sentimentalism in her makeup. Nevertheless, although far from the folk tradition in its genesis, Zhukovsky's ballad has been, as it were, absorbed into that tradition. The dream of Pushkin's Tatyana in the fifth chapter of *Evgeny Onegin* paraphrases motifs from Svetlana's dream. It is typical that in the actual image of the "silent and sad" Tatyana, the qualities of the ideal national heroine just enumerated are again dominant, and even the poetic quality of Pushkin's heroine is largely conditioned by the folklore atmosphere that surrounds her. In his portrait of Tatyana, Pushkin sketches her likeness with a direct reference to her charming predecessor, the epigraph to chapter 5 from Zhukovsky:

Dream no more such dreadful dreams,
Ah, my sweet Svetlana. . . .

(Pushkin, VI, 97)

The stylistic structure of this ballad is quite different from that of "Lyudmila": here, Zhukovsky is directly oriented toward Russian folklore, although he "ennobles" it in the spirit of Karamzin. His task is not to initiate any definite genre, but to revive the "popular spirit." Thus, "Svetlana" uses the style of a popular folktale (for

instance, the opening line "Once upon a Twelfth-Night Eve").
Legendary motifs permeate the whole work. The episode in the hut,
when the heroine finds herself alone with the threatening corpse,
was evidently suggested by a Russian folktale from the North, in
which a girl in a similar situation is helped by a cock (typically,
Zhukovsky turns the cock into a dove). Zhukovsky permits no trace
of folklore brutality in his treatment of the subject. In the story, the
theme of love is altogether absent (the girl sees her dead betrothed
as an enemy and sets out to outwit him, matching malevolent
cunning with cunning of her own); Zhukovsky's Svetlana is a model
of tender love; all other elements of the poem are subordinated to
the love interest, which, of course, can be traced back to "Lenore"
and "Lyudmila."

On the other hand, the ethnographical aspect of the customs and
traditions of the Russian people were brilliantly, if somewhat
conventionally, portrayed in such passages as the description of the
Feast of the Epiphany and the rites usually performed on that night,
inter alia. In the first two stanzas of the poem, approximately ten
different ways of foretelling whom one is going to marry are brought
in. Zhukovsky cites (in a slightly elaborated form) the original text of
a ritual song addressed to a mythical goldsmith. All this material has
been reworked, aestheticized, stylized. There is no denying that
Zhukovsky's "folklore" is only the starting point for a poeticized and
idealized conception of the spirit and life of the people. However,
the naiveté of the ballad is deliberate: the poet knows he is creating
a utopia. In "Svetlana," there is a concentration of "fair" fantasy
which overcomes the horror-fantasy of the original ballad, for all the
terrors and the brutality turn out to be a dream. Associations with
the earlier "Lyudmila" are a part of the calculated effect the author
wishes to make upon his readers.

The general tone of "Svetlana" is colored by sentimentalism,
but—unlike the typical sentimental tale—it is not monotonous, for
the author runs through a full range of folklore "registers." The
freedom with which Zhukovsky passes from one "register" to
another establishes distance between the author and the action,
whereas in the sentimental story the author is usually closely involved with the action in his capacity as a "sympathizer."

In "Svetlana," the author's attitude toward his subject is not a
simple one. He is simultaneously the detached onlooker, the
sympathizer, and the sage in whose voice there is a trace of a

scarcely perceptible amusement at the excessive naiveté of his sentimental heroine. Thus, in "Svetlana," we have the first experiment in a technique which Pushkin was to develop and refine: the multiple viewpoint of the narrator. Zhukovsky's irony—so unobtrusive as to be barely noticeable in "Svetlana"—was allowed freer play in his second work on a national Russian subject, "Gromoboy."

"Gromoboy" and "Vadim" combine to form the long ballad in two parts, "The Twelve Sleeping Maidens." Zhukovsky used the subject of C. H. Spiess' prose novel, *Die Zwölf schlafenden Jungfrauen.* Spiess' novel is based on Roman Catholic medieval legends of sinners who sell their souls to the devil and then, through religious penance, redeem their sin. In Zhukovsky's verse the subject of the novel undergoes a very considerable transformation. The poet took themes and incidents from Spiess, but peopled them with creatures of his own imagination.

In the creative history of "The Twelve Sleeping Maidens," an important part was played by the plan of a long historical poem to have been called "Vladimir," but which, in the event, came to naught. The poet, however, made extensive use in his ballad of materials he had prepared for this poem.

In "The Twelve Sleeping Maidens," Zhukovsky permits himself a liberty he had never taken in his translated ballads, however free the adaptation: he uses another author's subject matter as a quarry for the raw material to build an entirely original structure.

Retaining Spiess' basic idea of the purification of the soul through repentance and the redemption of sin, Zhukovsky gave his own imagination free rein in handling the details of the story. The action is set, not in medieval Germany, but in old Russia. The sinner's name—Gromoboy—suggests associations with the most distant, pagan Russian past. The name of the champion who rescues him—Vadim—is taken from the oldest Russian chronicle.

The connection with the plan for "Vladimir" is evident, first of all, in the introduction—for the first time in Russian poetry—of local color. This local color is still somewhat conventionalized, after the manner of the folk element in "Svetlana," but Zhukovsky nevertheless here adumbrated a new artistic principle that was to have a great future in the Russian Romantic poem. The ballad's action begins on the banks of the Dnieper, continues within the city walls of Novgorod, and several scenes are set in ancient Kiev, at the court of Prince Vladimir. The poet makes use of certain motifs from popular fantastic tales and from the *byliny*, the epic sagas of old Russia: the wandering of the hero, the hero's horse, the fight against a gigantic enemy, the rescue of the Kievan Princess, the refusal of the offer of her hand because the young hero is inspired by other, more heroic aims (the rescue of the true heroine).

An attractive feature of this ballad is the combination of lyricism, poetry, fantasy, local color, light irony, picturesque landscapes, and expressively rendered emotion: love, anger, terror, repentance, pardon. There are wonders and miracles, too, with the first part ("Gromoboy") devoted to horrific, infernal manifestations, and the second ("Vadim"), to the wholesome and the divine. All these various elements are harmoniously united in the light, free, elegant flow of poetic diction.

There is an attempt here at individualized character portrayal, particularly in the gloomy, autocratic Gromoboy, who has sold to the devil both his own soul and the souls of his twelve daughters. The demon who seduces Gromoboy is drawn with a touch of humor revealed in the "low" style with which he is—most expressively—portrayed.

> An old man with sharp, shining look,
>   And bushy beard unshorn,
> Bent double on a shepherd's crook,
>   With tail, and claws, and horns. . . .
>
> (II,87)

In other parts of "Gromoboy" the irony comes through in the hyperbolic treatment of horrors and sins on the one hand, and of absolute innocence on the other; in the playfully artless description of the appearance of twelve daughters, all in the course of one year. Zhukovsky does not, of course, equal the tongue-in-cheek humor of Pushkin that makes the latter's fairy tales such an enduring delight, but in this poem he is undoubtedly the precursor of it.

Almost always in Zhukovsky, but only in Pushkin's first poem, the fantastic element is devoid of popular coloring; the images of folk fantasy have been sublimated. This treatment derived not only from Zhukovsky's inability to make them seem real, but also from the necessity of distinguishing his own work from certain "low" genres that were becoming part of the past. For example, in the 1800s and

1810s, "comic" opera based on folklore motifs was still a fashionable genre, and here the element of the fantastic, deliberately coarsened and brutalized, was an important ingredient. Catherine II herself wrote one of the first Russian "comic" operas of the eighteenth century.

In works like these, the fantastic element was treated as one of the "lowest" degrees of the spiritual life. A typical example is provided by a "comic" opera Zhukovsky himself had written in his youth, entitled "Alyosha Popovich or the Terrible Ruins" ("Alyosha Popovich ili strashnye razvaliny," 1805–1808). The new Romantic age set Russian poetry the task of ennobling the fantastic element, and the first attempts in this direction naturally led to a certain sublimation.

While he was working on the "Twelve Sleeping Maidens," Zhukovsky wrote several lines in a similar style in a verse letter to Aleksandr Voeykov of 1814, "I bid you welcome, minstrel mine" ("Dobro pozhalovat', pevets . . ."). In these remarkable verses there is the same combination of jesting and elegance as in the "legendary-heroic" story. The stylistic standard established here by Zhukovsky was accepted by Pushkin in writing *Ruslan and Lyudmila.*

The second part of "The Twelve Sleeping Maidens," "Vadim," is distinguished by a more serious development of mystic motifs. The sinner and his daughters have been cast by God into an enchanted sleep; their castle is under a spell; several centuries pass before the appearance of their deliverer, Vadim. A mysterious, heavenly sound, as of bells, leads the youth on the long road from Novgorod to the forests of Kiev, where he succeeds in entering Gromoboy's enchanted castle. He falls in love with one of the sinner's daughters, seeing her only in the distance beneath a mysterious veil, and by so doing wakes them all from their magic sleep. The theme of mystic predestination, the call of the soul that overcomes time and space, this is the content the Russian poet treats here in all seriousness. The poetic, lyric quality of Zhukovsky's ballad has no parallel in Spiess' novel, which is full of rather crude erotic scenes. As even his contemporaries noted, Zhukovsky had made a far more chaste tale out of his ballad.

As for the local color of old Russia, this, too, Zhukovsky inevitably subordinates to aims he thought of as higher. Lyricism and mysticism pervade the story. Even in ballads, Zhukovsky remains true to himself. Naturally, lyrical elements are displayed most vividly in those ballads furthest removed from their foreign "model."

"The Twelve Sleeping Maidens" ends with a flight of poetic mysticism which becomes positively giddy in the last two verses.

> And seething hosts of seraphim
> In flaming depths are soaring. . . .

(II, 134)

These lines foreshadow Pushkin's "six-winged seraph" in his poem "The Prophet."

CHAPTER 5

The Medieval Ballad

Z HUKOVSKY's national-historic ballads are very closely connected with problems of Romanticism, but his ballads on medieval subjects are even more closely associated with the Romantic
movement. One of the most important poems of this cycle is "The
Aeolian Harp" (1814), written on an original subject. Zhukovsky
draws largely on his own imagination in portraying his characters in
the style of the Romantic concepts of the western European age of
chivalry.

First of all, it should be noted that it was precisely in his medieval, chivalric ballads that Zhukovsky developed his autobiographical
subject, something he did not do when working on Russian materials. It appears that in the latter he was more consciously aware of
the degree of artistic conventionality and stylization. Also, in
Zhukovsky's "Russian ballads" the theme of tragic love is missing;
here, with the exception of "Lyudmila," the closest to the foreign
original, the poet prefers "happy endings." This phenomenon,
though puzzling at first glance, may be explained by the orientation
of Zhukovsky's Russian ballads toward the Russian legendary
folklore which, in the best tradition of the fairy tale, invariably
requires a happy ending with a magical significance.

In the Romantic view, the human situation of unhappy love and
eternal separation was the major characteristic of the Middle Ages in
the West, and Zhukovsky shared this viewpoint. In the motif of
separated lovers itself, we have a symbolic incarnation of the
Romantic concept of the unattainability of the ideal.

Subjectivism pervades "The Aeolian Harp," a profound, personal
feeling that expresses itself through images of an "alien" world, far
distant in time and space.

In this ballad, the tragedy of forbidden love, which the poet
experienced with such immediacy, is clothed in the garb of "Os-

sianic" poetry. The Ossianic atmosphere is suggested first by the proper names—Ordal, Minvana, Morvena. (The last is the name of a country in one of the Ossianic songs.) The hero's name, Arminy (Arminius), is associated with ancient German history. With true inspiration, Zhukovsky combines gloomy "medieval" mystery with lyric emotion, tenderness, and harmony.

The central part of the text presents the scene of the lovers' meeting in the garden under cover of night and their dialogue, which in some of its features is reminiscent of the dialogue of Romeo and Juliet in Shakespeare's tragedy. This "duet" is very musical, thanks to the elegiac euphony and the rich organization of stanza and rhyme. The emotional quality of the scene is intensified by an elusive singing quality.

The love of the youthful pair, the poor minstrel Arminy and Minvana, the king's daughter, is defenseless in the face of the threatening forces of life. This defenseless quality is expressed by the touching simplicity of the subject, despite its Ossianic overtones. The action is somewhat static, for all Zhukovsky's passion and inspiration are expended upon the lyricism of this ballad.

Minvana and Arminy are among the most touching creations of Zhukovsky's love poetry, and are intimately associated with his elegies. The elegiac sadness for the transience of all earthly blessings receives a new psychological motivation. The ballad seems to say that love is tragic by its very nature: the stronger it is, the less can it be satisfied with anything short of eternity. Though nothing has yet occurred, the singer Arminy is already filled with prophetic foreboding. He expects and even desires death in order to transfer his love to eternity and thereby to ensure its security, impossible in this earthly life "lived in fear and trembling." As it turns out, the lovers' first meeting is indeed their last. Arminy is separated from Minvana and dies in exile. Minvana understands that he has died by the sound of the harp he left in her garden (a motif suggested by Friedrich Matthisson's "Lied aus der Ferne" and by Ivan Dmitriev's "The Lyre"). The sound of the harp is recreated with great virtuosity by the poetic words—"Pod*nialsia* pro*tiazhno* zad*um*chiv*yi zvon*" (literally: "and suddenly there sounded a long-drawn-out, thoughtful twang"); the whole scene is charged with muted but all-pervading emotion:

> Minvana sat grieving
> Beneath the wide branches . . . her soul elsewhere . . .
> And still was the evening . . .

> When suddenly . . . something caressed her warm hair;
>   And something came rustling,
>   Though breathless the night,
>   And something came plucking
> The harpstrings . . . unseen sweeping down from the height. . . .
>   (II, 78)

The ballad ends on a mystical note: the shades of Arminy and Minvana (for she is now dead too) fly over the familiar garden, the trysting tree welcomes them with a rustle of leaves, and the sound of the harp is heard once more.

In the "Aeolian Harp," as in Zhukovsky's other ballads and lyric poetry of this period, there are definite traces of Sentimentalism. In his translated "medieval" ballads, Zhukovsky sometimes makes use of the Sentimental style to suggest the naive, archaic quality of his originals ("Alina and Alsim," "Elvina and Edvin"). More often, however, the conventions of Sentimentalism suggest the "inner" world. In such instances the translator shows less aesthetic sophistication than his originals. This is particularly true of the early period; yet Zhukovsky's naiveté is not nearly so simple as it may seem. Zhukovsky is deliberately emphasizing, as it were, the specific features of the artistic element into which he is translating his foreign original. In this period he makes no attempt, as a rule, at exact translation in the sense that he is not so much interested in "informing" his reader about the original work *per se* as he is in grafting onto Russian literature a whole branch of kindred literature from western Europe.

The use of the Sentimental palette, at that time so much in vogue in Russian poetry, lent his free translations the appearance of being an organic part of the literature of his native land. This intention sometimes led him to simplify the more sophisticated ballads (Southey's, for example), but we should not forget that the Russia of the period from 1808 to 1814 was only just beginning to elaborate its own forms of modern poetry. In "Adelstan" (Southey's "Rudiger"), Zhukovsky, having outlined his heroine's physical appearance in rather general terms, proceeds to introduce a sentimental description of her spiritual qualities in the style of his own lyrical songs and romances:

> Midst the maids of Allen's Castle
> Laura shone in every part:

> For the eyes—a gracious angel,
> Sweet soul for the soulful heart.
>
> (II, 32)

In the original, the portrait is much more vivid:

> Was never a maid in Waldhurst's walls
> Might match with Margaret;
> Her cheek was fair, her eyes were dark,
> Her silken locks like jet.[1]

Not only the names are changed in "Adelstan," but the meter as well: where Southey uses a combination of three- and four-foot iambic lines the translation is in four-foot trochaic lines. The change produces a singsong quality which Zhukovsky had already employed to good effect to complement the folklore themes of "Svetlana," but of which there is no trace in the original.

The hero's new name, "Adelstan," is an assonance to Zhukovsky's name for the castle: "Allen" (in the original, Waldhurst Castle). The heroine, Margaret, becomes Laura. These euphonious, aestheticized names were more easily integrated into the Russian poetic element of the day than "Rudiger" or "Waldhurst."

. Southey took the subject for his ballad from the medieval German legend of Lohengrin, another version of which was later used by Richard Wagner as the basis for his opera. A sleeping knight is borne down the Rhine on a mysterious boat with a red sail, drawn by a swan. The knight awakes and lands at the gates of a castle whose beauteous chatelaine he woos and weds. The fascinating aura of mystery surrounding the knight, however, conceals a terrible secret: he is a sinner who has bound himself to deliver his firstborn to the Devil. At the critical moment, divine forces intervene on behalf of the mother and child and punish the sinner.

By softening the "local color" of the original, Zhukovsky leaves himself free to introduce certain Russian elements, albeit sparingly, with great artistic tact. Mention of the Rhine in the very first stanza sets the scene early and leads the reader to expect some tale of "chivalry"; in the second stanza Castle Allen is called just a castle, and then a *terem* (a word from Russian folklore, indicating any fair place of habitation or more particularly, the women's quarters of a great house); in the third verse, in the neighborhood of this "castle-

terem," we meet a band of "beauteous maidens" (*devy krasnye*) straight out of Russian folklore. These gradual transitions are effected with extraordinary skill.

The scene in the first stanza of the translation is as vividly set as in the original, and the artistic construction is even bolder. The words "day" and "Rhine," far from being mere designations of time and place, are made the operative substantives of the verse. In Southey we read:

> Bright on the mountain's heathy slope
> The day's last splendours shine,
> And rich with many a radiant hue,
> Gleam gaily on the Rhine.
>
> And many a one from Waldhurst's walls
> Along the river strolled,
> As ruffling o'er the pleasant stream
> The evening gales came cold.
>
> So as they strayed a swan they saw
> Sail stately up and strong,
> And by a silver chain he drew
> A little boat along.
>
> (Southey, I, 146).

In Zhukovsky's Russian:

> Den' bagrianil, pomerkaia,
>   Skat lesistykh beregov;
> Rein, v zareve siiaia,
>   Pyshen tëk mezhdu kholmov.
> On letuchei vlagoi peny
>   Zamok Allen oroshal;
> Terema zubchaty steny
>   On v potoke otrazhal.
> Devy krasnye tolpoiu
>   Iz rastvorchatykh vorot
> Vyshli na bereg—igroiu
>   Vstretit' mesiatsa voskhod.
>
> (II, 31)

Fading, the day reddened/ the slope of wooded banks;/ The Rhine, glistening in the sunset,/ flowed, luxurious, among the hills./ With the flying moisture of its foam/ it washed the castle Allen;/ the jagged walls of the tower/ were reflected in its stream./ Beauteous maidens in a group/ through the gates wide-flung/ emerged onto the shore—with their play/ to greet the rising moon.

The opening words *den' bagrianil* ("the day reddened") provide a very bold stroke of color. The *rastvorchatye vorota* ("wide-flung gates") and the *igra* ("play") by the light of the moon, add to the *stil russe* pastel effect which, incidentally, underscores Zhukovsky's usual tendency to invest his scenes with high poetry. The fairy tale element is absent in the original, where there are no "beauteous" maidens, nor any moonlight, but merely a variety of people from the castle strolling along the river bank, enjoying the cool evening air. Zhukovsky establishes a dreamy mood, disposing his reader to enter heart and soul into the wonders of his story rather than to regard it as an ethnographic, "alien" curiosity. For this reason it would be pointless to regret that Zhukovsky did not remain closer to Southey's original at that time.

On the whole, we may say that "Adelstan" is a very successful and effective variant of one of Southey's most Romantic ballads and, at the same time, a charming poem by Zhukovsky.

Southey's "Lord William," rendered by Zhukovsky as "Varvik" (1814), is altered in much the same fashion. Once again the names and place-names have been changed: Edvin instead of Edmund, Varvik instead of William, Avon instead of Severn. The verse structure is made more melodious. In the original, the rhythm (a four-foot iambic line with rhyme scheme *a b c b*) is very marked. Zhukovsky sets the first and third lines in iambic pentameters and makes them rhyme.

From beginning to end the text is rendered very freely. Three whole verses—an elegiac description of landscape—are added to the original.

No attempt whatsoever is made to "mingle" the "chivalric" and the style of the Russian popular ballad so prominent in "Adelstan," written only a year earlier. The verse is melodious, but not obviously singsong as in "Adelstan." Yet the ethnographical *realia* are again deemphasized. The translator seeks to convey the general atmosphere of the original without distracting detail which, by its very "exoticism," might well have intruded excessively upon the consciousness of the Russian reader of the time. This principle of

"softening" the local color was one that Zhukovsky was to continue
to apply in future, even in his most faithful translations.

Zhukovsky's primary concern was to convey to his readers the
meaning of the story as a whole, and of each incident in particular.
The theme of the slaughter of an innocent child drowned in the river
by a power-hungry baron again led the poet to employ the conventions of Sentimentalism. This treatment, however, was in no way
contradictory to the "message" of the original. The ethical pathos of
Southey's ballads, the subject of "retribution," was close to
Zhukovsky's heart and lost nothing in translation. The terror of the
murderer and his fearful end are powerfully portrayed.

Zhukovsky describes the episode at the river during the dreadful
flood of retribution in general terms. In the original, a crowd has
gathered on the bank, and to them the mysterious boatman addresses his cry: "My boat is small. . . ." In Zhukovsky's translation,
there is no crowd, but rather a series of scenes which mount in
intensity to emphasize the inevitability of the assassin's doom.

In places the translation is weaker than the original. For example,
Southey's magnificent lines:

> How horrible it is to sink
> Beneath the closing stream,
> To stretch the powerless arms in vain,
> In vain for help to scream!
>
> (Southey, II, 92)

are rendered by Zhukovsky as

> Vo mgle nochnoi on b'ëtsia mezh vodami,
> Oblit on khladom voln,
> Eshchë ego ne vidim my ochami,
> No on . . . nash vidit chëln.
>
> (II, 47)

In the gloom of night he struggles in the waters,/ he is drenched with the
coldness of the waves,/ we can no longer see him with our eyes,/ but he . . .
can see our craft.

The Russian poet, however, introduces a successful innovation in
his repetition of the first lines of the finale, which emphasize the
inherent, inevitable justice of the retribution: the same "silent

banks" hear the cry of the child at the ballad's opening and the cry of his murderer at its close.

In that same year of 1814 was produced one of Zhukovsky's masterpieces, his translation entitled "A Ballad Showing How an Old Woman Rode Double and Who Rode Before Her." The title is an almost word-for-word rendering of the original, although sometimes Southey's ballad is more briefly entitled "The Old Woman of Berkeley."

Southey's source was the English medieval chronicles, in which there are frequent digressions into legends about sinners and sorcerers who leave money in their wills to buy them the forgiveness of Heaven through masses to be said for their souls. A popular legend of this type is that of the witch of Berkeley, mentioned in a ninth-century chronicle. There are analogies in Russian medieval ecclesiastic literature and in old Russian and Ukrainian beliefs, which Gogol used in his story "Viy." Undoubtedly Gogol must have been greatly affected by Zhukovsky's ballad in which these motifs were, for the first time, given a brilliant literary form.

The "Old Woman" ballad occupies a special place in the poet's work. Its moral and ethical elements are not definitive here because of the complexity of the subject itself. In this poem, the fantasy lacks inner ties with the real problems of the life of the soul and seems to be an end in itself. Instead of his usual lyricism, Zhukovsky has recourse to a vividly ornamental style. He not only creates a virtuoso reproduction of the expressions and color of the original, but even rivals Southey himself in the vividness of his description of "horrors."

This translation is very free, beginning with the metric scheme of regularly alternating five- and four-foot iambic lines instead of Southey's free "tonic" verse. The verse structure has also been changed: Southey varies the number of lines in each verse from four to five or six.

Zhukovsky had adequate resources to reproduce the Romantic "horror" subject in a Russian setting. The strong meter emphasizes the dynamics of the story, the flocking together of satanic forces in their attack upon the Church.

As in "Lyudmila" and "Svetlana," Zhukovsky lent some parts of the ballad a more Russian sound. In one of the variants the title speaks of "An Old Woman of Kiev." The church service described is an Orthodox service; features of Russian folklore are introduced into the practices of the witch, who burns "the hair of brides" in magic fire. In Zhukovsky's story, the witch's son is made a monk-priest, or a celebate of the so-called "black" priesthood; in accordance with the Orthodox rite, he comes to offer the dying woman the "Holy Gifts," that is, the Sacrament, to hear her confession, and to give absolution. This moment, which complements the story as told in the original, is skillfully exploited by Zhukovsky to point up the antagonism between the divine and the Satanic:

> Yet when he brought the Host to her bedside
>   To comfort her as she lay dying,
> The crone in mortal terror groaned and cried:
>   "Stand off," she screamed, "From where I'm lying!
>
> Ah—do not bring the Holy Gifts so near
>   For they are for my torment now, not healing. . . ."
> And horrid was the sight of her white hair
>   And horrible her anguished breathing.
>
> (II, 48)

The description of the church where the old woman has been laid out in her coffin and of the prayers for the dead are all in accordance with Orthodox ritual. Icons, censers, priests, the Requiem, prostrations, deacons, and the very words used are all evocative of a Russian service.

> The deacons in their black dalmatics chant
> In mournful rhythms slow and solemn,
> Funeral candles burning in their hands
> And candles burn before the icons.
>
> . . . Before the altar still in sorrow bows
>   The monk with deep prostrations.
> The candle flames scarce touch the icons now
>   With tremulous illumination. . . .
>
> The cock had crowed . . . The fiends know well their hour
>   And, empty-handed, flee, defeated;
> More boldly chant the deacons from the choir,
> More boldly priests are prayers repeating.
>
> (II, 50–51)

This whole scene is so brilliantly original that even the creator of "Viy" could have learned something from it.

Typically Russian is the use of the word *vragi* (literally "enemies") for fiends, and the metaphor *lovitvy* (literally "the catch"), which bears strong Church Slavic overtones and has an oddly bookish, abstract and philosophical coloring. Both these expressions are most felicitous, and Zhukovsky uses them again in his account of the second night.

For this account Zhukovsky invents ever more new and expressive details. Instead of the monk and nun telling their beads, which would have been out of place in a description of Orthodox ritual, or the prayers of the fifty priests and the singing of the choristers, which have already been adequately conveyed in the preceding verses, we read:

> The monk lies *stretched in prayer upon the ground,*
>   The priests make countless deep prostrations,
> *The smoke from the spent candles wreathes around*
>   *The darkling icons'* watching-stations.
> The knocking's louder—fuller the bells chime
>   With sacred chants more urgent blending;
> *The singers' blood runs cold, darkness is in their eyes,*
>   *Hair stands on end, and knees are trembling.*
>
> (II, 51–52)

The italicized phrases have no equivalents in the original.

Sometimes, even when the translation is obviously striving to follow the original closely, Zhukovsky adds a few touches of his own, as, for example, in the lines:

> *The bells chime on, and still the deacons sing,*
>   And now the priests are *loud* in prayer,
> *The monk is weeping,* and the censers swing,
>   And brilliantly the candles flare.
>
> (II, 51)

In the original, this description consists of four parts: the chiming of bells, the prayer of the priests, the flaring of the candles, the telling of beads. In the translation, there are six parts, and an entirely new element has been added—emotion: "The monk is weeping." The adverb "loudly" which, in the original, begins this verse, is, as it

were, multiplied and magnified by the added motif of the deacons'
singing and the prayers read aloud. The verbs are all placed at the
ends of the lines, in the key positions, and this device increases the
dynamic quality of the scene. Zhukovsky also stresses the intensity
of the vigil.

The power of Satan struggling to burst into the locked church is,
in places, more forcefully suggested than in Southey:

> On the third night the candles are dim sparks,
>   The smoke is dense and smells of brimstone,
> In shadowy lines the priests stand in the dark;
>   The coffin through the murk looms dimly.
>
> The knocking's at the door: as though a brand
>   Had set the roaring ocean hissing,
> As though through desert steppe a storm of sand
>   On swarming wings went whistling.

(II, 52)

The ballad encountered emphatic difficulties with the censor. It
was first forbidden in 1814, but Zhukovsky made a second attempt
to print it in the mid-1820s under the new title of "The Witch." This
attempt, however, was no more successful than the first, for the
censor decreed that "the ballad 'The Old Woman,' now renamed
'The Witch,' must still be forbidden as a drama in which the Devil
triumphs over the Church, over God." In the end Zhukovsky had to
make radical changes in the lines which tell of the irruption of Satan
himself into the church and of his victory. The poet leaves Satan not
daring to enter the "church of God," standing in the shattered
doorway, nor is he permitted actually to lay hands on the coffin.
Chronologically, this was the last variant of the translation, but as it
is known to have been made under pressure, the text scholars accept as the fundamental reading of this part of the poem is as follows:

> And *he* appeared before them all aflame,
>   Ferocious, murky, furiously sudden,
> And God's great church glowed round him as he came
>   To red heat like a well-stoked oven.
>
> No sooner said he "Vanish!" than the chains
>   To dust and ashes were transmuted.
> No sooner stretched he forth his hand again,
>   The hoops beneath that hand had rotted.

> And so the coffin opened—and *he* yelled:
> "Arise and follow me, your Lord!"
> From the dead brow great drops of cold sweat welled
> Bedewing the still visage at his word.

(II, 53)

The image of Satan in the translation makes quite as grandiose an impression as in the original. Nevertheless, the individual peculiarity of Zhukovsky's ballad—which the censor quite failed to notice and which, indeed, is lacking in Southey's original—is the almost imperceptible humor of which we have already written in connection with "Svetlana." The function of this humor is protective: the reader does not altogether surrender to the horrors, which is the main difference between this ballad and Gogol's nightmarish "Viy." But Zhukovsky's touch is so light that this elusive, humorous reserve can only be felt in the Russian text. There is, for example, a hint of humor in the very use of the affectionate diminutive *starushka* in the title. *Starukha*, a form of the word devoid of such connotations, would have been a more exact rendering of Southey's neutral "old woman," and so from the very beginning, the effect of the word is faintly comic and reassuring against the terrifying setting of the ballad as a whole.

The translation is also richly sprinkled with vulgarisms: *vopit* ("yells"); *"d'iachki"* (here, a familiar diminutive for deacons); *popy* ("priests," a slightly pejorative vulgarism). In the Russian literary tradition, such words customarily indicated that fantastic happenings were not to be taken too seriously, as in the comic opera tradition we have already mentioned. All this is fully taken into account in Zhukovsky's "Old Woman" and exploited in masterly fashion. With the help of this nearly imperceptible gleam of humor the poet hints that his subject has its own conventions and draws a nice line of distinction between faith and superstition.

It is interesting that in one of Zhukovsky's own letters we find the following frankly jesting reference to the "Old Woman": "Yesterday I gave birth to, or rather adopted (since it was translated from the English), a ballad. Devils and graves galore! But it is the last I mean to do in this spirit. Don't think I mean to ride out into posterity exclusively on the backs of devils."[2] And indeed, "The Old Woman" marked the brilliant finale to Zhukovsky's ballads of the first period.

The second period has its own peculiarities. The Russian theme is now firmly separated from the western European. In work on medieval Western themes, the *couleur local* is intensified and no longer mingled with Russian touches. The elements of humor and the techniques of Sentimentalism have almost completely disappeared. There is less spontaneous lyricism now in the translations, but there are fewer concessions to the canons of light entertainment.

In this second period, Zhukovsky's idealization of the Middle Ages becomes intellectually more profound: the basic object of the translator's attention is the psychology of chivalry. His excursions into the fantastic assume a different complexion. Now Zhukovsky appears as the master of elegant, refined, knightly fantasy; his manner is distinguished from the manner of his earlier verse by a polished terseness and "aristocratic" reserve. Great inner tension is expressed in ennobled, refined, yet sufficiently vivid forms.

The poet no longer needs all the props of the "horror" ballads for his new objectives, and thus the importance of the fantastic element diminishes. In three ballads out of ten (Uhland's "Vengeance" and "Three Songs," and Schiller's "Rudolf of Hapsburg"), there is nothing of this nature at all. Zhukovsky selects for translation pieces in which moral problems of broad human significance are illustrated by material from medieval Europe. Romanticism itself, the yearning for the ideal, for the subtly supernatural, are represented as eternal qualities of the human soul ("The Knight of Toggenburg"). This was the period in which the spiritual approach to the Middle Ages so characteristic of Zhukovsky finally crystallized. This explains the fact, noted long since, that the translator now begins deliberately to dampen the colors and external effects of the original.

There can be little doubt that for many years Zhukovsky was guided by a desire to evoke associations for the Russian reader that would correspond not so much to the letter as to the spirit of the original. As Belinsky wrote, he was the translator into Russian "of the Romanticism of the Middle Ages,"[3] as it was understood by the Romanticism of nineteenth-century Europe. It was as though in each individual translation Zhukovsky had set out to integrate a whole movement. In his twenty-eight translations of "medieval" ballads he succeeded in concentrating the basic features of the vast and varied world of the western European Romantic ballad. Linked with this is the fact that some of these ballads are not, in the original, tales of chivalry, but Zhukovsky refines their whole tone and makes them such. This was what occurred in his translation of Goethe's "Erlkönig" ("Lesnoi Tsar' ").

It would be idle to maintain that all of Zhukovsky's alterations were improvements. For example, the "Erlkönig" translation, although extremely well known, is undoubtedly much weaker than the original, among other things because of the suppression of certain colorful, highly effective and striking details. Marina Tsvetaeva has made a fine analysis of this difference in her article "The Two Elf Kings."[4] However, when we examine this tendency of Zhukovsky's on principle, we must recognize its efficaciousness as a method of suggesting the Romantic conception of the age of chivalry. In western Europe, too, this conception was essentially a "lofty" one. The translator of the time was faced with a complex problem. He was obliged to take into account the specifics of Russian folklore: for example, a *tail* would have transformed his Elf King into a mere *leshii*, a vulgar wood sprite from a primitive legend. The idea of a wild and frightening, yet at the same time majestic and fascinating, sovereignty, so important in Goethe's original, would certainly have suffered. So Zhukovsky exchanged the tail for a beard.

In the ballad "The Eve of St. John" ("Zamok Smal'golm ili Ivanov vecher"), the crest on the shield of the mysterious knight is changed from a hound on a silver leash to three stars. A star is a symbol—one might even say a rather obvious symbol—of the exalted. A "dog," however, would have cued the Russian reader to a false chain of associations and most likely have summoned up a mental image of one of Ivan the Terrible's tough *oprichniki*, whose symbol was a dog's head in token of their willingness to savage the enemies of the tsar.

There is, however, no lack of bright color and expressive detail in Zhukovsky's ballads. About the time of the transition between the first and the second period, about the time he wrote "The Old Woman," his ballads cast off that monotony of style which had formerly been evident everywhere with the exception of "Svetlana." Pushkin's words on the "power and variety" of Zhukovsky's style are most applicable to the ballads of this period. To convince ourselves of this development, it suffices to compare ballads translated at different times: Uhland's "Die Rache" and "Harald" (both translated in 1816); Schiller's "Ritter Toggenburg" and "Der Graf von Hapsburg" (translated 1818); Goethe's "Der Erlkönig" and "Der Fischer" (translated 1818); and these, in their turn, with the translation of Walter Scott's "The Eve of St. John" (1822).

Zhukovsky's profound mastery of the original, "his recreation of it as a product of his own imagination," are intimately linked with the degree of freedom he permits himself as a translator. The ballads become more and more an organic part of Zhukovsky's lyric *oeuvre*, indeed become indistinguishable from it, and eventually, in the third period, replace his original lyric verse altogether.

The ballads of the second period, like the lyric poetry of that time, are full of Romantic mysticism on the one hand, and of Romantic pathos on the other. "Harald," "The Fisher," "The Elf King"—all envelop the reader in an atmosphere of mystery; he feels surrounded by supernatural powers holding a strange, enchanted fascination for him. In "Vengeance," "Three Songs," "Rudolf of Hapsburg" and "The Eve of St. John," the key to the conflict is man's free choice in his own conduct. The moral and religious elements are closely intertwined with each other in "Rudolf of Hapsburg," which deserves examination in more detail.

The first verse of the translation is so remarkably powerful and such a faithful rendering of the original that we can do no better than offer the Russian and German texts for comparison.

> Zu Aachen in seiner Kaiserpracht,
>   Im alterthümlichen Saale,
> Sass König Rudolphs heilige Macht
>   Beim festlichen Krönungsmahle.
> Die Speisen trug der Pfalzgraf des Rheins,
> Es schenkte der Böhme des perlenden Weins,
>   Und alle die Wähler, die Sieben,
> Wie der Sterne Chor um die Sonne sich stellt,
> Umstanden geschäftig den Herrscher der Welt,
>   Die Würde des Amtes zu üben.
>
> (Schiller, II, 252)

The Russian translator renders this superb verse as follows:

> Torzhestvennym Akhen vesel'em shumel,
>   V starinnykh chertogakh, na pire
> Rudol'f, imperator izbrannyi, sidel
>   V siian'e ventsa i v porfire.
>
> Tam kushan'ia reinskii fal'tsgraf raznosil;
>   Bogemets napitki v bokaly tsedil,
>   I sem' izbiratelei, chinom

Ustroennyi drevle svershaia obriad,
Blistali, kak zvëzdy pred solntsem blestiat,
Pred novym svoim vlastelinom.

(II, 142)

Aachen resounded with triumphant gaiety;/ at a feast in his ancient chambers/ sat Rudolf, the chosen emperor,/ in purple and the glow of his crown./ The Pfalzgraf of the Rhein served various dishes there;/ the Bohemian strained drinks in the goblets;/ and seven electors, properly/ carrying out the ceremony established of old,/ glittered, as stars before the sun,/ before their new master.

In addition, however, there are quite important divergences from the text of the original, though not at all because the translator has not fully understood some idea or found it too difficult to convey. For Schiller, worried by the fragmentation of Germany, the image of Rudolf of Hapsburg was important above all as the image of the just and strong unifier of his country. Zhukovsky altered the character of the hero, making him an altogether more humble and sensitive person. Here we feel the Russian poet's concern for the educational effect of his translation, not only upon the general public, but quite specifically, upon the Imperial family. (The translation was made in 1818 and printed in the collection *Für Wenige*.) Zhukovsky's Rudolf von Hapsburg is an elegant product of the ideal of chivalry; his speech is made gentler and more courteous than in the original.

Zhukovsky's *idealization* of the hero colors his entire translation. The ballad's central episode is Count Rudolf's meeting with the priest in the forest. So devout is Rudolf that he sets the priest on his own horse so that he may arrive more swiftly to comfort a dying beggar. Zhukovsky emphasizes the future king's veneration for this churchman whom he has met by chance.

Schiller has the count hand over the reins of his horse to the priest, whereas Zhukovsky makes him give the prelate a leg up, as though he were a groom. And in his dialogue with the humble servant of the church, Zhukovsky's future monarch outdoes his German prototype in humility. This and many similar touches throughout the translation direct the reader's attention away from the hero himself to those religious ideals which inspire him. This innovation explains yet another change by the translator. In Schiller's version the count finally merely relinquishes his claim on a horse that has been used in a holy cause; in Zhukovsky's, he symbolically "dedicates" the horse to God, a somewhat unorthodox act from the point of view of the church, but one that expresses the naive simplicity of the young knight's soul. An apotheosis of this faith is given in the following verse, without a direct parallel in the original:

> "But how could I dream," the count said with reserve,
>   Eyes lowered in civil observance,
> "That ever this horse for mere pleasure should serve,
>   That has been our Redeemer's good servant?
>
> If you, Holy Father, will not for yourself
>   Accept this good beast from my poor store of wealth
> Then give I it now from this hour
> To Him in Whose great gift is every good thing,
> Power, honor, and wealth, to Whose feet I would bring
>   This instant: life, honor, and power."
>
> (II, 144)

The increased authority of religion in the translation is automatically accompanied by an increase in the *authority of poetry,* insofar as the singer and the priest are the same person. Apart from this, Zhukovsky depicts the king as a conscious devotee of poetry as a high art, and not simply as a customary courtly entertainment.

Schiller's Rudolf proclaims merely that he does not intend to change his knightly habits, now that he has become emperor:

> So hab' ich's gehalten von Jugend an,
> Und was ich als Ritter gepflegt und gethan,
> Nicht will ich's als Kaiser entbehren.
>
> (Schiller, II, 253)

Zhukovsky, on the other hand, speaks specifically of the "sacred" habit of being a "friend" to "song" and of "bringing delight" to feasts with "minstrelsy":

> Ya pesnei byl drugom, kak rytsar' prostoi;
> Stav kesarem, broshu l' obychai sviatoi
> Piry uslazhdat' pesnopen'em?
>
> (II, 143)

I was the friend of songs as a simple knight; / now, as emperor, should I abandon my sacred custom / of sweetening feasting with song?

By contributing his own thought, Zhukovsky is not misinterpreting, but rather interpreting, Schiller. An example of this technique is the fifth verse. Magnificent both in the original and in the translation, Zhukovsky's rendition is a model of fidelity in the manner in which it conveys Schiller's thought with all the profundity of "coexperience" and power of expression—yet here too we find original motifs:

> It is not for me to command the bard's soul
>   (The ruler replies to the minstrel),
> A higher allegiance the minstrel doth owe,
>   For *his* overlord is the instant;
>
> The hurricane roars twixt the earth and the sky
> And who shall say whither or whence it doth fly?
> From caverns great rivers come seeping. . . .
> So songs in the depths of the soul are conceived
> And from slumbrous enchantment dark feeling is reaved,
>   To flame into music up-leaping.
>
> > (II, 143)

In the three last lines, with astonishing terseness, Zhukovsky has introduced a thought about the essence of poetry that has no counterpart in the original. The transformation of the "dark" (potential) into "leaping flame" (realization) is a metaphor that expresses Zhukovsky's understanding of the function of art as simultaneously creation and enlightenment. Schiller, by contrast, maintains that art brings inward, elemental feelings to the surface of consciousness.

The conception of the power of poetry that Zhukovsky offers in this translation made a lasting impression upon Pushkin. In "The Lay of Oleg the Foresighted" ("Pesnia o Veshchem Olege," 1822), the subject for which is taken from the Russian Primary Chronicle, the thought of the great power of poetry is carried further and we are shown poetry and political sovereignty in conflict. It is interesting to note that in Pushkin's treatment the chronicle story of the killing of the prince by his horse has something in common with "Rudolf of Hapsburg," where the tale of the horse is also at the center of attention. The confrontations of the sovereign and the priest in Schiller's ballad correspond to the confrontation between Oleg and the pagan priest or sorcerer. In "Rudolf of Hapsburg," the priest and the poet are one. In Pushkin's poem, we have the same idea: the functions of the pagan priest are syncretic: he has some of the features of a poet, and, more particularly, of Pushkin's own conception of the poet as prophet.

Pushkin's sorcerer utilizes poetic formulas reminding us of Zhukovsky's ballad, although it is characteristic of the older poet that he puts his thoughts on the freedom of artistic creation in the mouth of the sovereign and not in that of the priest-poet, as Pushkin does.

"The Lay of Oleg the Foresighted" is an attempt to create a national, Russian, Romantic ballad, and it is only natural that in this poem there should be some dependence on Zhukovsky. The careful reproduction of the meter of "Rudolf of Hapsburg" and (in abbreviated form) of the verse structure, render this dependence more obvious. However, in Pushkin's poem the confrontation between poetry and power is depicted as an unresolvable and fatal conflict.

In "Rudolf of Hapsburg" the details of the original have been retained with masterly fidelity. They convey the elegance and at the same time the "simple-heartedness" of the medieval world in such scenes as the description of the feast. On the other hand, in the translation of another ballad by Schiller, "Ritter Toggenburg" ("Rytsar' Togenburg"), material and psychological details are deliberately played down. For this treatment, too, there are definite reasons.

For the first time in poetry, in "Ritter Toggenburg" Schiller created images of the soul's longing ("Sehnsucht"), of the yearning for the ideal, for the unattainably beautiful. Zhukovsky had made this concept very much his own, and in his translation this ballad—one of Schiller's most Romantic—appears even more Romantic. The neutralization of local and historical color was one means of deepening the eternal significance of the images. Schiller uses real geographical locations such as "Joppes Strand." The tragic finale is to some extent decided by coincidence: the heroine has taken the veil only on the eve of the hero's return. Zhukovsky eliminates all this, leaving only the typical medieval theme of the Crusades (the knight goes to war in Palestine).

Moreover, in the translation the manner in which the feeling of love is expressed is rather different. It is made less individualized in order to grant the philosophical dimension higher visibility. Though he sacrifices certain expressive touches, Zhukovsky still succeeds not just in retaining the lyricism of the original, but even in intensifying it. Schiller's first verse reads:

> Ritter, treue Schwesterliebe
> Widmet euch dies Herz,
> Fordert keine ander Liebe,
> Denn es macht mir Schmerz.
>
> (Schiller, I, 72)

The translation of this verse, while remaining fairly close to the original, does not mention the heroine's "pain" on hearing the knight's protestations of love but, on the contrary, introduces the idea of the "sweetness" of sisterly love. The words "sweet" and "dear," given importance by their prominence at the beginning of the first two lines of the translation respectively and assigned to the heroine entirely on the translator's responsibility are definitive for the whole ballad as a hymn to platonic love:

> Sladko mne tvoei sestroiu,
> Milyi rytsar', byt',
> No liuboviiu inoiu
>   Ne mogu liubit':
> Pri razluke, pri svidan'e
>   Serdtse v tishine—
> I liubvi tvoei stradan'e
>   Neponiatno mne.
>
> (II, 137)

Sweet it is for me as your sister,/ dear knight, to be,/ but with another kind of love/ I cannot love you:/ At parting, at meeting,/ my heart remains calm—/ and the agony of your love/ is incomprehensible to me.

In the original, the last four lines read:

> Ruhig mag ich euch erscheinen,
> Ruhig gehen sehn;
> Eurer Augen stilles Weinen
> Kann ich nicht verstehn.
>
> (Schiller, II, 72)

Schiller's "The quiet weeping of your eyes" ("Eurer Augen stilles Weinen") is here much more expressive than Zhukovsky's "the suffering of your love" ("liubvi tvoei stradan'e"). Zhukovsky, however, is not merely making an ordinary simplification. In this case his reserve, his ability to "generalize," his "contempt" for the externally expressive, correspond completely to the ideal quality of his supremely self-denying heroes. The principal point is that Zhukovsky's "separation" (*razluka*) and "meeting" (*svidan'e*) are generalized emotional states that have a permanent and general human significance.

Schiller's knight reacts more impulsively to his lady's refusal. Zhukovsky emphasizes the specifically "courtly," platonic nature of his behavior—he does not embrace his beloved, but merely presses her hand.

The changes introduced by Zhukovsky do not always enhance the text: in the fourth verse, for instance, we find the hackneyed elegiac expression "where she flowers" (*gde tsvetët ona*), instead of Schiller's "where she draws breath" (*Wo ihr atem weht*). Here, however, is the ballad's culmination. The hero contemplates the convent that shelters his beloved. Zhukovsky conveys the religious tenor of the knight's love by changing Schiller's text. Where Schiller writes of the convent looking out from among gloomy lime trees, Zhukovsky speaks of a "holy" abbey "shining" amid the dark limes. This abbey is doubly holy for the knight, both for religious reasons and because it contains his beloved. By substituting the word "shone" (*svetilsia*) for Schiller's more prosaic "looked" (*sah*), Zhukovsky achieves a kind of triple symbol, which adds profundity to the image: the abbey shines amid the surrounding darkness, as a still more symbolic "holy retreat" and, finally, as a light in the lover's consciousness.

Schiller's knight does not look at the abbey. On the contrary, he gazes hour after hour only at the window of his beloved, until that window opens, until his dear one shows herself, bending forward calmly to look down into the valley, "angelically gentle." In Zhukovsky's rendering, the *realia* are again transformed into symbols (his influence on the Russian Symbolists is certainly not surprising):

> Blickte nach dem Kloster drüben
> Blickte stundenlang,
> Nach dem Fenster seiner Lieben,
> Wie das Fenster klang,

Bis die liebliche sich zeigte,
Bis das theure Bild
Sich ins Thal herunterneigte,
Ruhig, engelmild.

(Schiller, I, 75)

I dushe ego unyloi
Schast'e tam odno:
Dozhidat'sia, chtob u miloi
Stuknulo okno,
Chtob prekrasnaia iavilas',
Chtob ot vyshiny
V tikhii dol litsom sklonilas',
Angel tishiny.

(II, 138–39)

Here Zhukovsky introduces a more poetic epithet to describe the heroine (the Russian *prekrasnaia* suggests a loftier beauty than the German *liebliche*); in the line "chtob prekrasnaia iavilas'," instead of Schiller's "ins Thal hinunter" ("down into the valley"), Zhukovsky's heroine bends down "from the heights" ("ot vyshiny") and we feel that "height" is simultaneously indicative of the real situation of the convent and—to a still greater degree—the symbol of a lofty spirituality. The image of the "angel of stillness" is Zhukovsky's own creation, and he introduces the actual theme of "stillness" which, anticipated in the previous line by the epithet "still" in "Still valley"—permeates the whole finale. "Stillness," as we are aware, is a most characteristic Zhukovskian theme. It may well be that Zhukovsky's translation of "The Knight of Toggenburg" had a certain influence on Pushkin as the author of the poem "Once There Lived a Poor Knight-errant" ("Zhil na svete rytsar' bednyi"). All in all, Zhukovsky was particularly successful in his translations of Schiller.

In the ballad "The Eve of St. John" ("Zamok Smal'gol'mskii ili Ivanov vecher"), Zhukovsky rivals Walter Scott, the author of the English original. From the opening line the "local color" is laid on thick, for here the element of medieval "exoticism" is particularly important. The descriptive part of the translation is magnificent both in the material solidity of the word images and in their fidelity to the original.

The Baron of Smaylho'me rose with day,
He spurred his courser on,

Without stop or stay, down the rocky way,
That leads to Brotherstone.

Do rassveta podniavshis', konia usedlal
Znamenityi Smal'gol'mskii baron;
I bez otdykha gnal, mezh utësov i skal,
On konia, toropias' v Broterston.

(II, 151)

Rising before daybreak, the famous baron of Smaylho'me/ saddled his
steed;/ without stopping for breath, among cliffs and precipices,/ he drove
his horse, hastening to Brotherstone.

He went not with the bold Buccleuch,
His banner broad to rear;
He went not 'gainst the English yew
To lift the Scottish spear.

Yet his plate-jack was braced and his helmet was laced,
And his vaunt-brace of proof he wore;
At his saddle-gerthe was a good steel sperthe,
Full ten pound weight and more.

Ne s moguchym Bokliu sovokupno speshil
    Na voennoe delo Baron;
Ne v krovavom boiu perevedat'sia mnil
    Za Shotlandiiu s Angliei on;

No v zheleznoi brone on sidit na kone;
    Natochil on svoi mech boevoi;
I pokryt on shchitom, i topor za sedlom
    Ukreplën dvadtsatifuntovoi.

(II, 151)

Not with the mighty Buccleuch together did the baron/ hasten to the field of
battle;/ not in bloody conflict did he think to square accounts/ for Scotland's
sake with England./ But he bestrides his horse in iron armor; / he has
sharpened his warrior's sword;/ a shield covers him, and behind his saddle/
is fastened a twenty-pound ax.

The brooding, suppressed atmosphere of excitement is intensified
by the heavy meter (anapest) and onomatopoeia, and the hefty,
cumbersome word *dvadtsatifuntovoi*, which corresponds by its
position in the line to four, five or even six words in other lines of
the poem, and crashes down with all the weight of the battle-ax it

describes at the end of the verse. This effective device was not borrowed from Scott, who has six words in this line to Zhukovsky's two. The translator shows great skill in preserving internal rhymes. The lines we have quoted here are, indeed, among the most technically proficient Zhukovsky ever wrote. The meter and style of his version of "The Eve of St. John" were to serve as a model in all later Russian poetry for the translation of the English ballad.

In some places, Zhukovsky tones down the bright colors of the original. Thus, Scott describes the armor and accoutrements of the knight in great detail:

> His arms shone full bright, in the beacon's red light
> His plume it was scarlet and blue;
> On his shield was a hound, in a silver leash bound,
> And his crest was a branch of the yew.[5]

For this description Zhukovsky substitutes a verse of his own:

> Byl shelom s sokolinym perom
> I palash boevoi na tsepi zolotoi,
> Tri zvezdy na shchite golubom!

(II, 154)

A helmet with a falcon's plume/ and a broadsword on a golden chain,/ three stars on a field of azure!

The brilliant hues of the original (red, scarlet, and blue) are replaced by more symbolic ones (shining gold, azure); and for the more prosaic "silver leash," Zhukovsky substitutes a "golden chain." Since the hero of the episode is not a live knight, but a ghost returned from beyond the grave to haunt a woman he had loved when alive, it is not difficult to grasp the artistic motivation behind the rearrangement of the images.

Zhukovsky's treatment of the lyrical theme likewise differs from the original. Walter Scott's heroine says to her beloved, as she tries persuading him to meet her at a late hour:

> "Now, out on thee, faint-hearted knight!
> Thou should'st not say me nay;
> For the eve is sweet, and when lovers meet,
> Is worth the whole summer's day.

(27)

Zhukovsky's lady takes a loftier tone:

> O somnenie proch'! bezmiatezhnaia noch'
> Pred velikim Ivanovym dněm
> I tikha, i temna, i Svidan'iam ona
> Blagonsklonna v molchan'e svoyěm.

(II, 153)

> Ah, put aside doubt! the calm night
>   before the great day of St. John
> is quiet and dark, and is well disposed
>   toward trysts in its silence.

"Ah, put aside doubt," she exclaims, instead of the rallying "Now, out on thee." The "sweet eve" is replaced by "calm night." Zhukovsky himself introduces the expression "The great day of St. John," and the word "great," although in fact it applies directly to the "Day of St. John," colors the whole context and elevates the love theme itself. Suppressing the word "lovers," Zhukovsky dwells more on the night, which he pictures as being "quiet and dark," and "well-disposed in its silence." In the original, all that is said is "the eve is sweet."

In the last period of Zhukovsky's ballad writing, the choice of words for the group of "knightly" ballads allows him to create a generalized image of the Middle Ages. Zhukovsky creates this image as a complex whole, showing different facets of the world of the Middle Ages. In Uhland's "Durand" ("Alonzo" in the Russian), Southey's "Donica," and Thomas Campbell's "Lord Ullin's Daughter," he has shown us a specifically Romantic range of emotions through works on the subject of forbidden, unhappy love, a subject that he had made peculiarly his own many years before. In Schiller's "The Diver" he depicts the apotheosis of the limitless self-sacrifice of which love is capable.

Southey's "God's Judgement on a Wicked Bishop" ("Sud Bozhiy nad Episkopom"), Scott's "The Gray Brother" (translated as "Pokaianie"), and Uhland's "Der Waller" ("Bratoubiitsa") are gloomy, dramatic ballads of sin, retribution, and redemption. Here the Middle Ages are shown as a world in which men lived by ideas of the polarity of earthly and heavenly forces, a polarity which, however, did not exclude close contact between them. The mysticism of Southey's "Queen Oracca and the Five Martyrs of Morocco" borders on superstitious fanaticism. In Uhland's "Roland Schildträger" ("Roland-Oruzhenosets"), on the contrary, the same period is painted in more optimistic colors and depicted in its aspect of simple-hearted, ennobled, and life-affirming heroism. The motifs of folklore, legend, and superstition are found in Uhland's "Junker Rechberger" (translated as "Rytsar' Rollon") and in the new, more literal translation of Bürger's "Lenore."

An example of the quintessential Zhukovsky is the handling of Uhland's ballad "König Karls Meerfahrt" ("Plavanie Karla Velikogo"), where the basic subject is a kind of demonstration of various types of medieval chivalry (the portraits of the twelve peers).

Finally, the very essence of the Romantic conception of the Middle Ages, in its most inspired form, is revealed in the translation of Uhland's "Graf Eberhards Weissdorn" ("Staryi rytsar' ").

The style of these translations is richly varied, as the range of their subjects requires. It is not surprising that Zhukovsky sometimes returns to the colors of his early palette. His naive version of "Lord Ullin's Daughter" reminds us of "Elvin and Edvina," and his "Rytsar' Rollon" of "The Old Woman Who Rode Double. . . ."

The third period is distinguished by an infallible feeling for measure and style. The Russian balladic style had been Zhukovsky's own discovery and, in the early period, it was only natural that it should have been influenced by certain native styles, including sentimentalism and the use of lexical and syntactic archaisms. By now Zhukovsky had polished this, his own balladic style, to a truly classic dignity. This accomplishment was undoubtedly rendered possible also by Pushkin's parallel achievement. Having himself received so much from Zhukovsky, Pushkin began, from the middle of the 1820s on, to be a model of poetic diction, spontaneous and perfect, for the older poet.

During this period Zhukovsky created his supremely authoritative translations of "medieval" ballads: "God's Judgement on a Wicked Bishop" and "The Beaker" (he translated Schiller's "Der Taucher" as "Kubok"). Here he attained the height of achievement in the art of translation as spontaneous, creative work.

It would seem that not Zhukovsky, but Schiller, Southey, Uhland, and Walter Scott themselves had rewritten their ballads in Russian. However, just as before, Zhukovsky is not the slave of the text: inspiration and a sense of measure suggest original variations. In "God's Judgement on a Wicked Bishop," the length is slightly increased—there are eighty-eight lines instead of seventy-six. From four lines of Southey's, Zhukovsky has made eight, extending the description of the bishop's impregnable palace. In "Roland the Shieldbearer," Zhukovsky suddenly perceives the possibility of weaving a metaphor out of one simple phrase, and he does not deny himself the pleasure of doing so. In Uhland's poem the giant, clambering down the mountain, crashes to the ground; in the translation, the giant himself is seen as a mountain ("He came crashing down like a black mass of earth"). In the same poem, a man "standing before the castle" is depicted as "staring out of the window and thinking," an image conjuring up a more vivid picture and, in the context, a more telling chain of associations.

In "Queen Oracca and the Five Martyrs of Morroco" ("Koroleva Uraka i piat' muchenikov"), Zhukovsky introduces a certain ecclesiastical eloquence that corresponds very well to the contents of the ballad.
Instead of:

> And they departed to the land
> Of the Moors beyond the sea

We have:

> I v Afriku smirenno ponesli
> Nebesnyi dar ucheniia Khristova
>
> (II, 199)
>
> And they humbly bore off to Africa
> The sacred gift of Christ's teaching

Other examples would not be difficult to find.

In "The Fratricide" (Zhukovsky's translation bears the Russian title "Bratoubiitsa," whereas the Uhland original is called "The Pilgrim"—"Der Waller"), the ascetic self-torment of the penitent is heightened. Instead of chains clanking on his arms and legs, Zhukovsky has the "bitter chain" drawn tight about his "bleeding legs." Here, too, we discern far more subtle changes: in place of the depiction of the Holy Virgin, who "shines there like a golden guiding star," we have the simpler but more effective lines "From that steep cliff, upon the waters/ Looks the Mother of Our Lord" (II, 218). In the finale Zhukovsky creates a new symbolic image of death as liberation. Where Uhland has, "But the soul is already free, she reigns in a sea of light," Zhukovsky writes: "And the soul has flown away/ To the city of freedom—and God . . ." (II, 220).

In this mature period, Zhukovsky acquired an increasing mastery of symbolism. In "The Old Knight" (Uhland's "Graf Eberhards Weissdorn"), the title has acquired a symbolic meaning. The anonymity of the knight suggests that the story's importance does not lie merely in what happened in one definite, individual case, and this anonymity is preserved in the text. The "whitethorn" of the German title is replaced by an olive bough, rich with associations with the Holy Land. The finale, too, suggests new associations not contained in Uhland's original, which reads:

> Der Herr war alt und lass;
> Das Reislein war ein Baum,
> Darunter oftmals sass
> Der Greis in tiefem Traum.

> Die Wölbung hoch und breit
> Mit sanftem Rauschen mahnt
> Ihn an die alte Zeit
> Und an das ferne Land.[6]

Zhukovsky's rendering of the finale would become the direct source of Lermontov's "A Bough from Palestine" ("Vetka Palestiny"):

> Nad nim, kak drug, stoit,
> Obniav ego sediny,
> I vetviami shumit
> Oliva Palestiny;

> I, vnemlia ei vo sne,
> Vzdykhaet on gluboko
> O slavnoi starine
> I o zemle dalekoi.

(II, 217)

It stands above him like a friend,/ embracing his gray hair,/ and with its branches rustles / that olive tree of Palestine; / And, sensing this in sleep,/ he sighs a deep sigh / for the glorious days of old / and for a distant land.

"Alonzo" (1831), Zhukovsky's version of Uhland's "Durand," is the freest of his later ballad translations. It represents his artistic

credo at this period. It is, in fact, an original and extremely refined
variation on a theme. The whole sound structure of the ballad has
been altered. Where Uhland's line has a trisyllabic meter with
pause substitutions, Zhukovsky used a four-foot trochaic line with
feminine endings throughout (the "Spanish" rhythm). In the interests of euphony, the names have been changed, "Durand"
becoming "Alonzo," and "Blanka," "Izolina." The peculiarly musical
quality of the translation is not only well suited to the subject of the
ballad (a minstrel's love), but also to Zhukovsky's treatment of this
subject, more subtle and symbolic than Uhland's. Assonances follow
one another in unbroken rhythm to express the mystic harmony of
loving hearts. The orchestration of the vowels is exceptionally
skilled. The absence of rhyme, compensated for by the rich assonances, emphasizes the hidden, profound musicality of the text.
The key to Zhukovsky's text are the phonemes *iz, e* and *n,* which
play on the names of the hero and heroine almost as though the
whole ballad were an anagram on "Alonzo-Izolina." Yet this is done
very subtly. There is no sense of artificiality or strain to mar the airy
quality of the verse.

> *Iz* dal*e*koi Pal*e*stiny
> Voz*v*ratias', pevets Al*on*zo
> K zamku Bal'bi probliz*h*al*s*ia
> Po*l*on *pesn*ei vdokhn*o*ven*n*ykh:
>
> Tam krasavitsa m*la*daia
> Struny zvon*k*ie podsl*u*shav,
> Obomleet, zatrepeshchet
> *I* s al'tana vzor naklonit.
>
> O*n* prikhodit v zamok Bal'bi,
> *I* pod oknami poët on
> Vse, chto serdtse molodoe
> Vtaine vydumat' umelo.
>
> > > > > > > > > > > > > (II, 181)

From far Palestine returning
Came the minstrel, young Alonzo,
Homeward came to Castle Balbi
Singing songs of inspiration.

From the keep a lovely maiden,
Heard the twanging of his lute-strings,

> Trembled at the sound, half-swooning,
> From the lofty altan gazing. . . .
>
> Now he comes to Castle Balbi,
> And he sings beneath the windows
> All that youthful souls in secret
> Are well able to conceive of. . . .

In the original there is no mention of Palestine, and the two last lines with their complex psychological perspective correspond to the much simpler German "Was er süssestes ersonnen" ("the sweetest things that he had dreamt of").

The very structure of Zhukovsky's verse conveys an impression of the supreme spiritual sensitivity that is the gift of love. For him, this forms the basis of the subject, in which the hero is in a permanent state of transition from one sphere of existence to another—either from life to death, or from death to life. Zhukovsky adds an original verse of his own to demonstrate how easily such a transition can take place:

> Even as the sudden stirring
> Of the air can quench a candle,
> So was quenched the youthful minstrel
> From one word untimely spoken.

(II, 182)

The least hint of the sensual would have detracted from the artistic effect Zhukovsky sought to create, and accordingly he replaced the "tenderness" and "longing" of the heroine as the song calls her back to life with "amazement" or "wonder," playing again on an eloquent correspondence of sounds: Iz*ol*ina—iz*uml*en'e ("wonder").

It is as if Zhukovsky were striving to reproduce the very sounds of the music of those "heavenly spheres" through which Alonzo seeks his beloved. At the end, too, Zhukovsky adds a verse to Uhland's finale, thereby riveting our attention upon the final, fateful misunderstanding: Alonzo dies from the death of Izolina as Izolina is restored to life by Alonzo's song. Thus the last verse poses a new problem. This lack of correspondence in the fate of the two lovers is—paradoxically—the result of the harmonious attunement of their two souls: the inner power of their love is proportionate to its outer defenselessness. Furthermore—and this is most important—Zhukovsky accentuates the impossibility of complete union with the beloved beyond the grave. As we know, this motif had a profound, personal significance for him. And in spite of all that he had said and written, Zhukovsky shows here how completely vain he considered such illusory hopes to be. Zhukovsky introduces the motif of the echo as the only answer man can receive to his questions about justice and immortality:

> Round him stretch the heavens, shining
> Beautiful and all untroubled. . .
> And, by a vain hope deluded,
> Flying through their blessed spaces,
>
> Calls he loudly: "Izolina!"
> Passionless the call reechoes:
> "Izolina! Izolina!"
> Through the blest, unanswering spaces.
>
> (II, 182)

The Russian word *blazhenstva* (literally "blessednesses") is here an exact equivalent of the German *Seligkeiten*. The plural of this word is very rare in Russian, but Zhukovsky uses it twice in his translation as compared with Uhland's once. It introduces a new motif: Alonzo "flies through" the "blessednesses," whereas Uhland's hero merely "sees" them. This underlines the feeling of space in the word "blessednesses"—indeed *blazhenstva* and *prostranstva* have a similar sound.

The indifference of the heavens is heightened. The blessed spaces of heaven are "untroubled," "unanswering"; Alonzo's cry, full of earthly tragedy, is transformed into nothing, into the "passionless" sound of the echo. The theme of "empty" ("desert") "blessednesses" is also to be found in Uhland ("die öden Seligkeiten"), but in Zhukovsky's translation it is greatly intensified and carried much further by the introduction of the "echo." These blessed spaces become a universal emptiness through which the beloved's name echoes in vain.

CHAPTER 6

The Ballad and the Ancient World

OF Zhukovsky's thirty-nine ballads, the seven written on ancient subjects stand out. One of these—"Achilles"—is entirely original; the others are translations from Schiller. They are almost equally distributed over the second and third periods.

The early "classical" ballads—"Cassandra" ("Kassandra," 1809), "The Cranes of Ibycus" ("Ivikovy zhuravli," 1813), and "Achilles" ("Akhil," 1812–1814)—bear the unmistakable imprint of their time. Here we find ourselves once again in the pre-Pushkin period, in the time of Zhukovsky's youth and Batyushkov's best work. Then, antiquity was still a live topic: interest in it was maintained both by the traditions of Classicism and by the new, Romantic ideas.

The ancient world still held a magnetic attraction for artistic thought of that time. Batyushkov's "neoclassicism" had much in common with German eighteenth-century `neoclassicism, with its conception of antiquity as a definite historical stage in the development of mankind (Winckelmann, the "Weimar Classicism" of Goethe, Schiller, and Hölderlin). At the beginning of the nineteenth century in Russia, the new understanding of antiquity was being propagated by Aleksey Olenin, the president of the Academy of Arts: Batyushkov and Zhukovsky were both frequent guests in his salon. The influence of Olenin's circle also extended to Nikolay Gnedich, translator of *The Iliad*.

For Batyushkov, antiquity represented an ideal of harmony between man and the world about him. The classic idea of antiquity as a norm, as a model worthy of imitation, was transformed by Batyushkov into a Romantic dream, a kind of Utopia of whose unreality he was himself well aware. But Batyushkov built his model of the ancient world from purely literary images and echoes (the lyrical subjects of Ovid, Horace, and Tibullus). True to the literary canons of the time, he often treated ancient themes in a Sentimental spirit, a kind of Empire style in literature, as Boris Tomashevsky has written.[1]

Zhukovsky was interested in antiquity less as an ideal than as a point in the history of mankind where ever relevant human problems and conflicts could be seen in concentrated form, as essences. Nevertheless, he still introduced a considerable amount of Sentimentalism in his treatment of ancient heroic subject matter, even though it was not so well suited to sentimental elaboration as the medieval. Zhukovsky's Cassandra is more naive than Schiller's: Zhukovsky transforms the austere prophetess into the lyrical heroine of a melancholy Russian early nineteenth-century elegy. The dread gift of prophecy is presented in the guise of elegiac premonitions of early death:

> And in vain my lamentation,
>   And my sorrow seems disgrace;
> My lone heart its desolation
>   Pours out to the desert wastes.

(II, 15)

In this poem, Zhukovsky employs a number of lexical and syntactic archaisms that convey not so much the archaic quality of the world he is depicting as the archaic quality of the translation.

On the other hand, Zhukovsky also wrote powerful verses containing concentrated, aphoristic formulas saturated with emotional and rational content:

> Shall I save them if I tell
> Horrors that must come to pass?
> Ignorance—true life doth spell,
> Knowledge—spelleth death to us.
> Phoebus, seal mine eyes again—
> Take this dreadful gift from me;
> It is terror, mortal pain
> Vessel of thy truth to be.

(II, 16)

Here the expressiveness of Schiller's "Nimm, o nimm die traur'ge Klarheit/mir von Aug' den blut'gen Schein" ("Take, oh take the grievous foresight,/the bloody glow before mine eyes") is much diluted, though the reproduction of the antitheses in the third and

In its interpretation of the ancient world, "Achilles" is akin to the tragedies of Vladislav Ozerov, a Sentimentalist reformer of the Russian classic theater ("Oedipus in Athens," 1804; "Polixena," 1809). Ozerov's Oedipus has much in common with Zhukovsky's Priam, the father of Hector, slain by Achilles. "From his cheeks with purple mantle/The poor monarch wipes his tears—" (II, 66). In these two lines Zhukovsky gives an elegantly laconic formula for the whole of Ozerov's theater.

Batyushkov wrote that Zhukovsky "had made a Fingal of Achilles."[2] The Fingal to whom he refers, one of the heroes of Ossian-Macpherson, was likewise the subject of a tragedy by Ozerov.

Batyushkov's poem "Friendship" ("Druzhestvo," 1811–1812) springs from a literary impulse similar to that which inspired "Achilles." Batyushkov gives us a more sculptured and vital figure in his Achilles, possibly because his poem was based on an ancient model, the ancient Greek of Bion of Smyrna.

Before finishing "Achilles" in 1813, Zhukovsky began work on his translation of Schiller's ballad "Die Kraniche von Ibycus," but this work is already distinguished by elements of the style of Zhukovsky's later and more perfect classical ballads. As opposed to "Cassandra" and "Achilles," in "The Cranes of Ibycus" Zhukovsky pays close attention to the details of ancient rituals and beliefs.

At the foundation of the ancient Greek legend that Schiller chose to use for his ballad is the classical notion of retribution. Schiller introduced a new motif—the influence of art on the human soul. Both these themes were profoundly congenial to Zhukovsky.

According to the legend, the ancient Greek poet Ibycus (sixth century B.C.) was slain on the way to take part in a ritual bardic competition, and he is depicted both by Schiller and by Zhukovsky as representing simultaneously the type of the ancient bard and the eternal type of the poet. Zhukovsky makes a great effort to convey the vitality and mood of the original as well as its plot structure; including especially the central episode in which the assassins, watching a performance of Aeschylus' *Eumenides* before a great audience, lose their self-control and betray themselves. Additional forcefulness is introduced into the scene of the procession and chorus of the Erinyes:

> With *blazing eyes* around they thronged
> And in *wild* chorus raised their song
> That *stabbed* the heart with dreadful fear.

(II, 40)

The words underlined have no equivalents in the original. The description of the Erinyes is given with an effective variation. Instead of snakes and adders blowing out their venom-swollen bellies, as in Schiller, Zhukovsky has them making their forked tongues quiver with a hissing sound and displaying a terrible row of fangs.

The impression produced by the chorus of Erinyes upon the spectators is also intensified. Schiller's malefactors seated in the front rows actually see the flying cranes; in Zhukovsky's translation, they only hear their approaching cry.

An important variation in the sense of the text is the substitution of "a pitifully moaning voice" for "the terrible clamor" of the cranes at the scene of the murder. It makes the cranes more than mere witnesses to fate. Their moaning expresses sympathy, and to a certain extent even solidarity with the poet. The word "moans" (*stony*) is used of both the poet and the cranes. Here Zhukovsky is playing on the symbolic notion of the poet as a bird. In the finale, the flying birds bear away with them, as it were, a part of Ibycus' being.

This half-expressed association that shimmers so elusively through the verse is essentially Romantic, but then Schiller, also, albeit in quite different ways, tended to romanticize antiquity.

In Zhukovsky's later translations of classical ballads the sentimental element has given way to a more generalized concept. Nevertheless, these later translations simply demonstrate how essential "Cassandra" and "Achilles" were as stages in the evolution of Zhukovsky's balladic style. Zhukovsky is always inclined to modernize the ancient world, more than does Schiller. And this predisposition, in certain important aspects, had its justification, not as a means merely to acquire a firmer grasp of a culture of the distant past, but as a means of establishing direct spiritual lines of communication with this past.

The concept of an unbroken development and the idea of the unity of the fates of mankind which accompanied it constituted, of course, Schiller's triumph as poet, historian and thinker. Zhukovsky lends this concept emotional conviction, but always retains in his "antique" style a wholly contemporary attitude. In "The Triumph of the Victors" ("Torzhestvo pobeditelei," 1828); "The Ring of Polycrates" ("Polikratov persten'," 1831); "The Eleusinian Feast" ("Elevzinskii prazdnik," 1832), wherein the Sentimental point of view no longer dominates, the modernizing spirit is still alive, owing to a certain responsive intensity of soul, to the comparative softness of tone, more suited, as Zhukovsky believed, to the taste of modern man, and to the endeavor to "poeticize" all the concepts involved.

These three features are typical of Zhukovsky's "ancient" ballads. In the way he combines and varies them lies the key to the originality of his approach to the material.

The *contemporary* criterion of humanism is definitive both for the sense and the style of Zhukovsky's "ancient" ballads. For him, humanism was an essential precondition to modern man's accepting any other culture as akin to his own way of thinking. This belief explains why Zhukovsky took it upon himself to tone down passages describing the cruelties or coarse customs of ancient times.

In the translation of "The Triumph of the Victors," he was faced with the problem of expressing Schiller's idea, which, in its turn, derived from the ancient notion that victors and vanquished are equally responsible before the supreme truth. In Schiller's poem, the victors themselves are wholly imbued with this philosophic resignation and hence are not lacking in humanism. Even so, Zhukovsky could not accept Schiller's ballad exactly as the latter wrote it. Schiller's description of the despair of the captive Trojan women—pale, their hair dishevelled, beating their breasts and lamenting—did not conform with Zhukovsky's system of philosophical harmony. So Zhukovsky provided the reader a totally different image, quite devoid of suffering:

> Crowding close along the strand
> Trojan women—spoils of war—
> Pass to quit their native land
> Captive led to lands afar.
> Wild the victors' paean of joy
> Mingles with their quiet lament
> For thy sacred splendor, Troy,
> Thy great glory, all forespent.
>
> (II, 157)

Here, Zhukovsky condensed the details of the original; and the two last lines are entirely his own. He also avoids any mention of the Greeks' plunder. Zhukovsky ennobles the victors, on the assumption that otherwise the contemporary reader will find nothing in them to arouse his sympathy.

The sarcastic tone of the original with respect to the old man, Nestor, who takes it upon himself to comfort Hecuba for the loss of her son, is not reproduced. Schiller's old reprobate lets his tongue run away with him somewhat and delivers the same speech twice. Zhukovsky did not consider such lofty matters a fitting subject for jest, and translated Nestor's speech on a perfectly serious, though simple, plane.

Thus, verse by verse, Zhukovsky remodels the text. The constant emphasis upon generalizations is accomplished at the cost of weakening the empirical element; this treatment is an important characteristic of Zhukovsky's text, and is done deliberately. If we compare individual verses in the translation with the original, the wealth of detail often leads us to prefer Schiller; yet the overall effect of the translation is as powerful as that of the original.

Zhukovsky increases the number of philosophical aphorisms, a technique fully in harmony with the structure of Schiller's ballad (the alternation of two voices, one of which fulfills the function of an ancient "chorus").

Here is one of the verses spoken by the "chorus" in the original:

> Drum erhebe frohe Lieder
> Wer die Heimat wieder sieht.
> Wem noch frisch das Leben blüht!
> Denn nicht alle kehren wieder!
>
> (Schiller, II, 260)

Therefore raise joyful songs,/you who will see your homeland once again./ You for whom life is still blooming fresh!/ For not all return to home!

Zhukovsky's rendering is as follows:

> Schastliv tot, komu siian'e
> Bytiia sokhraneno,
> Tot, komu vkusit' dano
> S miloi rodinoi svidan'e.
>
> (II, 158)

Happy is he for whom the glory/ of life has been preserved,/ he to whom it is given/ to see once more his beloved homeland.

This emotional charging of rational generalizations, achieved by Zhukovsky so successfully in "Cassandra," becomes here, in the translation of "The Triumph of the Victors" as in his other "ancient" ballads, a primary principle of style. Zhukovsky constructs the entire translation as a chain of aphorisms, antitheses, and ethicophilosophical observations; yet they are brimming with that complex poetic emotion which we have been discussing in the previous chapters. While preserving the basic meaning of the original, Zhukovsky contrives to be at once more aphoristic and more emotional. Thus in the German we have:

> Ohne Wahl vertheilt die Gaben,
> Ohne Billigkeit das Glück;
> Denn Patroklus liegt begraben,
> Und Thersites kommt zurück.

Without choice, the gifts are distributed,/without equity, good fortune;/ for Patroklus lies buried,/ And Thersites comes home.

Zhukovsky has:

> Skol'kikh bodrykh zhizn'poblëkla!
> Skol'kikh nizkikh rok shchadit! . . .
> Net velikogo Patrokla;
> Zhiv prezritel'nyi Tersit.

(II, 159)

How many vigorous men's lives are withered!/ How many of little worth are spared by fate!/ The great Patroclus is no more;/ The despicable Thersites lives on.

The additional antitheses of "the vigorous" and "those of little worth," "the great" and "the despicable" are entirely the work of the translator. And thus, in Zhukovsky's translation, the aphorism becomes a quotable generalization, as in his rendering of:

> Tapfrer, deines Ruhmes Schimmer
> Wird unsterblich seyn in Lied;
> Denn das ird'sche Leben flieht,
> Und die Todten dauern immer.

(Schiller, II, 262)

Zhukovsky translates:

> Slava dnei tvoikh netlenna;
> V pesniakh budet tsvest' ona:

Zhizn' zhivushchikh neverna,
Zhizn' otzhivshikh neizmenna.

(II, 160)

The glory of thy days will never fade;/ in song it will ever blossom:/the life of those who live still is uncertain,/the life of those who have lived is unchanging.

The word "to flower" (*tsvest'*) as applied to life has here been transferred from another part of the original, already quoted above. Most importantly, the sense of the aphorism has become absolute, owing to the fact that the antithesis fills the whole space of the verse, as it does not in the original. The antithesis is especially emphasized by its construction upon words of identical root or similar form: *zhizn'–zhizn'*; *zhivushchikh–otzhivshikh*; *neverna–neizmenna*; ("life–life"; "living–lifeless" [or, more precisely, "those who have already lived out their allotted span"]; "uncertain-unchanging"). In four words out of six, the root "life" is repeated, and the other two words are identical in form. This is only one of the brilliant innovations of a great poet.

Three more translations from Schiller—"The Ring of Polycrates" ("Der Ring des Polycrates"), "The Lament of Ceres" ("Klage der Ceres"), and "The Eleusinian Festival" ("Das Eleusische Fest")—confirm the perfection thus attained. Zhukovsky ceased to write ballads when he was at the height of his powers; so far as we know, "The Eleusinian Festival" was the last ballad he ever attempted. Here the translation occasionally attains such an astonishing degree of fidelity to the original as to be quite acceptable by standards of accuracy applied only to prose translations. Sometimes Zhukovsky introduces features of the Homeric style lacking in Schiller's original, for example, in the use of compound epithets. In 1828, three years before writing "The Eleusinian Festival," he had translated some fragments from *The Iliad* and was now making use of this experience.

Zhukovsky's interest in this particular ballad by Schiller in which the evolution of citizenship is shown in a series of effective episodes, was undoubtedly closely associated with the thoughts expressed in Zhukovsky's journalistic writing, with which we are already acquainted.

In sum, we may conclude that Zhukovsky looked with greater

optimism upon the fate of humanity in general (the theme common to all his "classical" ballads) than he did upon the earthly lot of the individual human being. This view, however, was only to be expected, given his philosophy of life and the whole tenor of his thought.

CHAPTER 7

Epic, Drama, and Tales

I *The Epic*

IN his translation of the epic, as with the ballad, Zhukovsky sought to solve two problems with an equal sense of responsibility: to recreate the text of a foreign original in the Russian language, and to make verse with a structure similar to that of the original. In our day the question of whether poetry translations should correspond to the originals in the actual form of the verse is no longer a matter of debate. This was not always the case. In the time of Zhukovsky's youth, argument waxed hot as to whether it was desirable to translate Tasso into Russian in octaves, or Homer in hexameters. Doubts about this sprang not from any lack of veneration for Tasso or Homer, but, on the contrary, from a general feeling that the Russian language was an insufficiently subtle instrument to render their work. Zhukovsky was one of the first to take a stand against this lack of faith in his native tongue. For him, the choice of verse form was always decided by the original, with the exception of those cases where the author himself might be considered a free "adaptor" of some subject from world literature. In such instances, Zhukovsky labored in accordance with another principle: he selected a form corresponding to the nature of the subject.

The impulse for Zhukovsky's first epic translations was obviously the polemics which sprang up over the use of the hexameter in Gnedich's translation of extracts from the *Iliad* (the earliest publication was in 1813). By 1814, Zhukovsky had already translated in hexameters the second canto of Friedrich Klopstock's *The Messiah* (retitled *Abbadona* in the Russian).

This translation is of double interest—both as the first experiment with a "demonic" subject in Russian poetry and as one of the early examples of the Russian hexameter. The hexameter seemed to Zhukovsky to be an entirely fitting form for the "sacred" biblical

142

subject, for it was at once ancient yet of general significance for all humanity. The first sketch for Zhukovsky's own poem, "The Wandering Jew" ("Vechnyi zhid") (on which he began work in 1831 and to which he returned not long before his death), was also written in hexameters. In the later fragments of this poem, as in the adaptations of "The Story of Joseph the Beautiful" ("Povest' ob Iosife Prekrasnom," 1845) and "From the Apocalypse" ("Iz Apokalipsisa," 1850–1851), Zhukovsky shifted to a more neutral, narrative, unrhymed iambic pentameter.

As an attempt to transplant epic verse to Russian soil and produce a model for a modern, national epic, Zhukovsky's *Abbadona* was not markedly successful. The poet's conciliatory interpretation of the myth of the fallen angel and the artificiality of the genre of the "new" classical epic were largely to blame for this failure.

A few years later the "demonic" theme was taken up once again in Russia, this time in the protestant, freedom-loving variant stemming not from Klopstock, but from Byron (the "Demon" of Pushkin and Lermontov). In his translation of Thomas Moore's "Paradise and the Peri" ("Peri i Angel," 1821), the second part of the poem *Lalla Rookh*, Zhukovsky also returned to the "demonic" theme, though still in its conciliatory aspects.

Two years after *Abbadona*, in 1816, Zhukovsky again employed the hexameter in his translations from Hebel: "Der Karfunkel" ("Krasnyi karbunkel" or "The Red Carbuncle"), and "Das Habermuss" ("Ovsianyi kisel'" or "Oatmeal Porridge").

The originals are written in hexameters in one of the German dialects (Swabian). Long before his translations from Homer, Zhukovsky had begun to work out two types of the hexameter: the heroic, and the narrative-conversational. The hexameter seemed to him a potentially universal form and, indeed, he himself used it with remarkable mastery to obtain the most varied effects.

In the preface to his "Red Carbuncle," Zhukovsky wrote: "The translator of this folk tale . . . wished to discover, first, whether it is possible for this attractive simplicity that is so precious an attribute of poetry to be made native to Russian poetry? and second, whether the hexameter, which has hitherto been devoted solely to the significant and lofty, will prove suitable for the telling of a simple tale? While not considering his experiment successful, he does think that both the one and the other are possible. As to the story that he offers here to the reader, it is translated almost word for word."

Zhukovsky was attracted by the narrative-conversational hexameter as one of the possibilities of developing the "simple" narrative style of verse in Russian. At the same time it was important for him that the hexameter ennobled the everyday contents of such verse, lending an almost "ritual" significance to the most ordinary facts of life ("Oatmeal Porridge"). Zhukovsky's interest in Hebel was by no means a first step toward greater realism, for idealized simplicity is the very opposite of "natural" simplicity. For the nineteenth century this course would not be fruitful: the narrative function was already inevitably destined to pass from poetry to prose.

Zhukovsky did not confine his use of the narrative-conversational hexameter to those instances where he was translating from originals using this meter. Such was his rendering of Adelbert von Chamisso's *Undine* (1831–1836), and of four tales in verse in 1831: "Two There Were and Then One More" ("Dve byli i eshchë odna" from Southey and Hebel); "The Fight with the Dragon" and "The Judgment of God" ("Srazhenie s zmeem" and "Sud bozhii"—both from Schiller); and "Neozhidannoe svidanie" ("Unexpected Meeting," from Hebel).

Zhukovsky's earliest "heroic" hexameter was a translation from book XI of Ovid's *Metamorphoses*, "Ceyx and Halcyone." On the whole, Zhukovsky conveys the original very faithfully, although in places the words used to express the emotions are somewhat modernized (the introduction of the epithet *milyi*—"dear one," among others). In 1822 the poet translated the second canto of Virgil's *Aeneid*, titling it "The Fall of Troy." Up to this time Virgil had been translated into Russian only in prose or in Alexandrines. Zhukovsky's model translation of Virgil was an excellent preparation for his own subsequent translations of Homer.

However, to the extent Zhukovsky was himself a Romantic, he was interested in Romantic works. The Russian Romantic poem, whose destinies were at that time the subject of much debate among both literary critics and writers, could not make independent progress until Russian literature had assimilated the experience of Byron at least to some degree. The supreme achievement of the Russian Preromantic narrative poem, Pushkin's *Ruslan and Lyudmila*, oriented as it was toward Ariosto, Voltaire, and Ippolit Bogdanovich, was the brilliant, crowning achievement of the old tradition rather than the discovery of a new genre. "Who in Russia can read English and write Russian?" the temperamental Vya-zemsky demanded. "I am ready to pay him with my life for every line of Byron!"[1] By this, of course, he meant translations of not merely "informative," but "creative" significance.

At the end of 1821 and the beginning of 1822, Zhukovsky trans-lated Byron's "The Prisoner of Chillon." By this time Pushkin had also become interested in Byron's poetry via French translations and was writing the first Russian Byronic poem, "The Prisoner of the Caucasus" ("Kavkazskii plennik").

Pushkin worked independently of Zhukovsky's translation but, subsequently, the latter's version of "The Prisoner of Chillon" was to have a decisive influence on the actual model of the Romantic poem in Russia. The monologic structure of the "confession," the concentrated, monotonous, inflection, which is organically linked with the peculiarities of the meter, formed the mold for Lermontov's poems "The Confession" ("Ispoved' "), "Orsha the Boyar" ("Boiarin Orsha"), *Mtsyri*, etc. This translation of Zhukovsky's was a milestone in the history of Russian literature. Of "The Prisoner of Chillon" in Zhukovsky's rendition Belinsky wrote: "Our Russian singer of quiet sorrow and melancholy suffering has found in his soul firm and powerful words to express the terrible, subterranean torments of despair sketched by the lightning brush of the titanic poet of England."[2] The verse construction of "The Prisoner of Chillon" consists essentially of rhyming couplets with masculine endings in a four-foot iambic meter. Byron, however, does not adhere strictly to either meter or rhyme scheme: in his poem we find lines of only three feet, feminine rhymes, alternate rhyming, and even three rhyming lines in sequence. Zhukovsky translated the whole poem into Byron's basic form, rhyming couplets with masculine endings in a four-foot iambic meter.

In Byron's poem it was not so much the theme of freedom that attracted Zhukovsky as the theme of human experience, brotherly tenderness and love. At the same time that Zhukovsky was making his translation from Byron, and quite independently of both the English poet and his Russian translator, Pushkin was working on his poem, "The Robber Brotherhood" ("Brat'ia-razboiniki"). Of this poem Pushkin wrote: "Some lines remind one of the translation of 'The Prisoner of Chillon.' This is my misfortune. The correspon-dence between my work and Zhukovsky's is quite accidental, my fragment was written at the end of 1821."[3] Zhukovsky slightly deemphasized the freedom-loving, political meaning of Byron's original and intensified the lyrical element. Thus, to the depiction of the younger brother's death he added the lines: "Upon the post like a spring flower. . . / Upright he hung with drooping head." In the last line of the poem the hero's indifference to the freedom he has at last won is deepened: where Byron has "Regained my freedom with a sigh," Zhukovsky writes "I sighed for my captivity."

Zhukovsky left untranslated the prologue to "The Prisoner of Chillon," that hymn to freedom, the "Sonnet on Chillon." Byron himself knew of Zhukovsky's existence and called him the "Russian nightingale."

It was no accident that, in the years between 1810 and 1820, questions involving epic and dramatic verse forms became so urgent. At that time verse was still firmly linked to genre; in many ways, to choose this or that verse form was paramount to choosing this or that point of view on one's subject. If the translation of the "Prisoner of Chillon" opened the way for the monologic "confession"—poem (the first exponent of this form before Lermontov was Kozlov; after Lermontov, it was used occasionally by both Nekrasov and Ivan Turgenev), then the translation of Schiller's *Maid of Orleans* was an important event in the history of the Russian theater. Conceived as early as 1812, the translation was actually made in the period from 1817 to 1820.

As in the eighteenth century, up to the very beginning of the 1820s the "French" alexandrine classic verse form had dominated Russian drama, making it virtually impossible to create new dramatic characters or situations. Zhukovsky translated Schiller's *The Maid of Orleans* in the meter of the original: in rhymed iambic pentameter with optional caesura and frequent enjambments. This form was subsequently (particularly in the 1830s) widely employed in Russian verse drama and facilitated its emancipation from the canons of French Classicism.

Zhukovsky first used it in 1818 in his translation of a dialogue of Hebel's entitled "Mortality" ("Tlennost' "). At the time, the experiment met with scant sympathy and was even parodied by Pushkin in an epigram. The verse seemed too prosaic; yet in drama it provided great freedom. Later Zhukovsky was to use the verse form of *The Maid of Orleans* in his "dramatic tale" "A Norman Custom" ("Normandskii obychai," 1832), translated from Uhland, and in his translated "dramatic poem" *Camoens* (1839).

Almost at the same time as Zhukovsky, Vilgelm Kyukhelbeker, too, set out to reform Russian dramatic verse in his original tragedy, *The Argonauts* (*Argiviane*, 1821–1824), which was written in unrhymed iambic pentameter. However, the traditional caesura lent the verse a bookish, classical sound that both Zhukovsky and Schiller had succeeded in avoiding.

In his tragedy *Boris Godunov* (1824–1825), Pushkin chose a verse form akin to Kyukhelbeker's, but later considered his retention of the classic caesura to have been a mistake in this "Shakespearean" tragedy from the history of his own people.

It was typical of Zhukovsky that he should have smoothed over some of those features of Schiller's "Romantic tragedy" most closely connected with the inevitable heritage of Shakespeare's theater (details of everyday life, historical background, transition from the lofty to the "low"). Zhukovsky followed his translator's instinct, which prompted him to convey the dominant quality, the constructive principle of the work, and, by the same token, its unique individuality—Zhukovsky concentrated the reader's entire attention upon the image of Joan herself, her enthusiasm, her moral and religious ideal. He reproduces the character of Joan with veneration and inspiration, not omitting a single detail, or shade of meaning. On the other hand, he tends to play down the more "Falstaffian" lines of dialogue not important for the action and not really characteristic of Schiller himself (the terms of abuse the English heap upon Joan; such expressions as "the witch of Orleans," "that loose Circe," and "the crow's mother" in reference to Queen Isabeau).

The mounting tension of Joan's mood through all her speeches is superbly rendered—her prophecy, her farewell to the motherland, her prayer in the scene of the king's capture.

In his translation Zhukovsky subtly calculated all those additional overtones it would be possible to introduce from the Russian literary milieu.

Where he does depart from the original, however, his action can quite often be explained on political grounds for reasons of censorship. For example, his translation of *The Maid of Orleans* is subtitled "A Dramatic Poem" and not "A Romantic Tragedy," as Schiller called it (the censor feared the connotation of free thought inherent in the word "romantic"). Every reference to the question of the accession to the throne, as well as the whole relationship between Charles VII and his mother Isabeau, sounded thoroughly "dangerous" in Russia. For, only two decades before, with the connivance of his son Alexander I, Paul I had been assassinated; and Paul's father, Peter III, had been dethroned and condemned to die with the full knowledge of his own wife, Catherine II. Certain facets of Isabeau's character and her moral laxity might have evoked undesirable associations—undesirable not only from the censor's point of view, but also from that of Zhukovsky himself. The poet had no desire to see his tragedy—of which the most important feature was the apotheosis of the most sacred and ideal aspects of human personality—understood as a drama à *clef* with allusions to current politics.

At the same time, nonetheless, Zhukovsky intended that his *Maid of Orleans* should convey a "message" to his contemporaries living under the conditions of Russian political life. It was not by chance that he had planned this translation in 1812, when his mind was filled with the events of the Napoleonic invasion. In Russia, *The Maid of Orleans* had, as it were, a twin political target: Zhukovsky perceived it as being an "exhortation" to Tsarism, on the one hand, and to the people of Russia on the other. The Russian poet did not share Schiller's political viewpoint and republican sympathies. He slightly ennobled the figure of Charles VII (although allowing him to remain insignificant enough) and omitted those passages in which Schiller had painted a particularly telling picture of the Queen Mother's cynicism and dissolute way of life.

In spite of all this, the theatrical censor prohibited performance of the tragedy. In 1824, in connection with the *Maid of Orleans*, an official edict even forbade the performance of any plays in blank verse.

Zhukovsky's translation is still the accepted standard for all editions of Schiller published in the Russian language. It would indeed be impossible to improve on Zhukovsky's translation. The passages Zhukovsky himself deleted are usually restored in translations by other poets.

II   Undine. *Translations from Oriental Epic Poetry*

The Maid of Orleans and "The Prisoner of Chillon" marked the end of that period of the development of Russian literature when translations had constituted one of the most important elements of the literary process. Thanks in no small degree to Zhukovsky, a true marriage between the new Russian culture and the culture of western Europe had at last been effected—the process of organic assimilation was complete. The epoch was approaching when a knowledge of the artistic discoveries of Russian literature would become an essential part of the cultural background of the western European reader.

It was therefore natural that Zhukovsky's choice of poems for translation should now assume a more subjective character. The poet concentrates on what is particularly close to him, not necessarily taking the demands of the time into account. In this category fall almost all the above-mentioned stories in verse written between 1831 and 1832, including Walter Scott's "Marmion" (translated as "The Subterranean Trial"—"Sud v podzemel'e"), la Motte-Fouqué's *Undine*, "Camoens," and "Two Tales" from Chamisso and Friedrich Rückert. On the other hand, he undertook monumental, "academic" translations of ancient epics which possessed a significance above and beyond the demands of the moment.

The best translation of the first type was *Undine* (1831–1836). As in many of his ballads, Zhukovsky here perceives as an eternal need of the human spirit a belief in a spiritual dimension of wonder, a belief which has its being both within us and "just around the corner" from us. This is the basic thought, the hidden pathos Zhukovsky introduces into la Motte-Fouqué's prose legend. The very fact that the prose was translated into verse, and not just into verse, but into hexameters, had wrought a transformation of the whole content of the work. While adhering closely to la Motte-Fouqué's text, Zhukovsky lends the story an added depth of perspective. Zhukovsky's narrative-conversational hexameter, although very simple in tone, free, and never monotonous in description, nevertheless bears the ineradicable imprint of its provenance: loftiness of spirit. The poetic animation of Zhukovsky's narrative style is tinged with sadness, which, as the tale unfolds, assumes poignant, psychological reality (the emotion of Undine when she loses the affections of her beloved, the renewal of his love and his death). Zhukovsky's *Undine* is a rare combination of psychological verisimilitude with refined, reserved exaltation and symbolism.

The tone of the digressions and of the author's remarks is changed. La Motte-Fouqué stylizes these comments in the spirit of a naively artless storyteller of the olden days. In the translation, on the contrary, the voice of the storyteller is Zhukovky's own, with all the depth of lyricism and understanding of the human heart that always distinguished him. Many lines of *Undine* are worthy of occupying a place among the most exquisite of Zhukovsky's lyric poems, for example, the introductions to chapters 12 and 16.

Between 1837 and 1841, Zhukovsky labored over an adaptation of a fragment from the great Indian epic, the *Mahabharata* ("Nâla and Damayânti"). In this "Indian tale," as Zhukovsky called it and also in the "Persian tale" of "Rustem and Zorab," composed in the years 1846 and 1847 (from the Persian epic, Firdusi's *Shah-Namah*), he included only the most dramatic and emotionally moving episodes. Both these works are translated, not from the oriental originals, but from the German adaptations by Rückert (Zhukovsky had no knowledge of the Eastern tongues). Like Rückert in his "Nâla and Damayânti" Zhukovsky does not recreate the authentic form of ancient epic verse because of the profound differences in the language structure. Rückert chose the old German, short-line verse for his adaptation; Zhukovsky, his narrative hexameter. By the very choice of this meter, the "Indian tale" was drawn into the orbit of western culture. Paradoxical as it may sound, the hexameter did in fact achieve a thinly disguised modernization of the text (we have already discussed the essence of this technique in connection with the "ancient" ballads). Zhukovsky introduces elements of Christian thinking into the image of his hero, who is possessed by the evil one (the Indian evil spirit, "Kali," is called the "tempter" and the "impious" one). The whole text of "Nâla and Damayânti" is illumined with the lyrical reflection of Zhukovsky's original introduction.

In "Rustem and Zorab," Zhukovsky handles Rückert's text still more freely, but at the same time he attempts to convey the specific artistic quality of his oriental model. Here, Zhukovsky does not have recourse to the hexameter, feeling it to be out of place. "Rustem and Zorab" is written in free blank iambic verse (most of the lines are short). Rückert, however, was very much closer to the original in his six-foot iambic meter with its double and triple rhyme schemes.

Zhukovsky adds some episodes, all of which are profoundly tragic in tone: the description of the feelings of the dead hero's mother; the scene in which the horse takes leave of his dead master; the appearance of the beautiful Hudapherid by the body of the dead youth; the scene in which the dying Zorab recognizes his father;

Rustem's mourning for his son—all these episodes are informed with powerful dramatic tension. The style of Zhukovsky's translation closely approaches that of the Romantic poem. In this interest in subjects from the Indian and Iranian epos, there was an important element of Romantic fascination with the Orient. This preoccupation was also, however, closely linked with Zhukovsky's persisting interest in epic poetry and verse form throughout this later stage of his development.

III   The Odyssey

As a translator of ancient epic poetry, Zhukovsky's crowning achievement was his rendering of Homer's *Odyssey* (1842–1849). Now a poet of great experience and standing, Zhukovsky felt he had the right to undertake this work although he did not know Greek and it was too late in life for him to learn it. Here, however, Zhukovsky could not countenance the idea of a free translation. At his request the German Hellenist, Professor Karl Grashof, made a highly specialized crib with three "layers" of text. Zhukovsky describes this arrangement as follows: "He copied out the whole of the *Odyssey* for me in the original; under each Greek word he wrote a German word and under each German word the grammatical sense of the original. In this way I could have before my eyes all the literal sense of the *Odyssey* and the exact order of the words; in this chaotically exact translation, incomprehensible as it would have been to an ordinary reader, there were, so to speak, gathered before me all the raw materials of my building; all that it lacked was beauty, order, and harmony."[4] To achieve the latter was, as Zhukovsky wrote, his task.

He accomplished it conscientiously and steeped himself profoundly in the spirit of Homer's verse, grasping the basic principles of Homer's style through his own poetic intuition and the guidance of qualified specialists. The poet formulated his conception of the Homeric style in various letters, and then again in the foreword to the first edition of the Russian *Odyssey*: "Homer's poetry does not have single, striking lines but a continuous flood of them that must be caught whole, in all its plenitude and light; it is necessary to preserve every word and every adjective, yet at the same time to forget all particulars for the sake of the whole. . . . In translating Homer, one must renounce all affectation, all decorative adornment, all striving after effect, all coquetry. . . ."[5]

Zhukovsky also hoped that Homer would be accepted by the Russian reader not only as a great foreigner, not only as a representative of the ancient world, but that he should also become the eternal contemporary and even, almost, the "compatriot" of his readers. As always, Zhukovsky defined his task as the search for the commensurate rather than the literal. His *Odyssey* is modernized in vocabulary, in emotional tone, and in the descriptions of everyday *realia* and customs.

Zhukovsky always aims at simplicity, which he strives to achieve not only by cultivating the artless styles of the ancient rhapsodies, but also by adopting manners corresponding to his readers' sensibilities. He held that for the inhabitants of ancient Greece, the style of the *Odyssey* was easily accessible. Zhukovsky made it easier for his reader to understand Homer by eliminating his "philological" and "archeological" cast. This approach distinguished his translation from Gnedich's rendering of the *Iliad*: Gnedich filled his translation with rare, dialect terms seldom or never used in ordinary conversation, and preserved an archaic atmosphere with the help of ancient Russian and Church Slavonic words.

Zhukovsky cultivated a patriarchal "artlessness"; Gnedich, the lofty, heroic style. But Gnedich also modernized the ancient epic after his own fashion, stressing the theme of freedom as it was understood by his contemporaries, and attributing to people of the ancient world modern conceptions of nobility, generosity, and morality. The principle of russification distinguished both Zhukovsky's and Gnedich's translations from the German poetic translations of Homer, which were oriented toward a more literal rendering of the ancient Greek text.

As was his custom, Zhukovsky set special store by everything that was connected with the realm of the sentiments; he introduces his customary shades of meaning and accents in his depiction of marital fidelity and love, of parental and filial love, in his images of the heart's longings and the joys of reunion. All across the immense range of the text of the *Odyssey*, a new stratum gradually grows and spreads: small deviations in particular instances accumulate so as to effectuate a general shift of perspective. Apart from this, Zhukovsky's understanding of the ancient world was not free of errors, the most serious of which was his conviction that the antique view of life was necessarily a melancholy one stemming from the notion of the irretrievable passing of life.[6] Hence derives the atmosphere of romantic sadness permeating his *Odyssey* as a whole. Of the stylistic digressions from the original, worthy of note is the frequent transformation of the precise statements of the original into complex paraphrases (for example, instead of "he slept" we have "peacefully he partook of sweetly healing slumber"). The number of compound epithets is greatly increased. In all that concerns the texture of the verse, Zhukovsky evinced extraordinary virtuosity and the most painstaking care. It suffices to say that Gnedich, in his translation of the *Iliad*, made use of trochaic substitutions in roughly one out of five lines; in Zhukovsky's *Odyssey*, the ratio is one to one hundred.

After *The Odyssey*, Zhukovsky undertook to translate the *Iliad*, and completed two cantos.

IV *Tales*

From the distinguished folklore specialist, Aleksandr Afanasev, a statement has come down to us that Zhukovsky intended to devote the rest of his life to this translation of the *Iliad* and, as a parallel task, to the retelling and publication of folktales of various peoples of the world.[7] Legendary epos attracted him no less than the heroic. Zhukovsky was inclined to consider these two genres essentially akin: he saw even Homer himself as something in the nature of an inspired but simple-hearted spinner of tales.

Thus from Zhukovsky's standpoint, the monumental heroic epos and the artless folktale appeared not as identical, but as related forms. It is pointless to discuss here the rights and wrongs of this attitude, in depth. What is important to us, however, is the fact that this conviction lies at the very root of our poet's work on the folktale. It is also associated with Zhukovsky's view of Homer as a representative of primitive poetry, and with his concept of something common to all humanity and fundamental to the essential nature of all peoples, individuals, and art itself.

Of the six tales written by Zhukovsky between 1831 and 1845, three (which we will examine further on) were written in the spirit of Russian folktales: "The Tulip Tree" ("Tiul'pannovoe derevo") is an adaptation of a German story from the collection of the brothers Grimm; "Puss-in-Boots" ("Kot v sapogakh") is a French tale from the collection of Charles Perrault; "The Battle of the Mice and Frogs" is an ancient Greek parody of heroic epos, the "Batrachomyomachia."

The title of the first "Russian" folktale was deliberately ornate:

"The Tale of Tsar Berendey, of His Son Ivan-Tsarevich, of the Cunning Ploys of Koshchey the Deathless and of the Wisdom of Marya-Tsarevna, Koshchey's Daughter" ("Skazka o tsare Berendee, o syne ego Ivane-Tsareviche, o khitrostiakh Koshcheia Bessmertnogo i o premudrosti Mar'i-tsarevny, Koshcheevoi docheri"). The starting-point for this poem, written in competition with Pushkin, was Pushkin's own notes on the stories told by his nanny, the legendary Arina Rodionovna. Pushkin's own contribution was his "Tale of Tsar Saltan" ("Skazka o Tsare Saltane").

Pushkin's objective was to reproduce the type of the genuine folktale, an aim he achieved with brilliance. Every folktale of Pushkin's is, as it were, a working model assembled according to folk technique and from folk materials.

Zhukovsky's aim was different. What is specifically national in Zhukovsky's story is simply a veneer, whereas the entire essence of Pushkin's tale is the picture it gives of the mentality of the Russian people.

Zhukovsky's "Tale of Tsar Berendey" is also based almost exclusively on materials from Russian folklore, but at the same time it is written in hexameter. Zhukovsky, more often even than Pushkin, introduces traditional stylistic formulas and turns of phrase proper to folklore, but the general atmosphere of his poem is nevertheless *not* that of a Russian folktale.

Zhukovsky diverges from the truly popular element in his very point of view on life; this is evident in the way he depicts his hero and heroine. The theme of the wise maiden, the sea-king's daughter, and of the hero's magic flight with her, so popular in Russian folklore, is given a literary gloss, and the characters are "ennobled." The type of the "wise maiden," a favorite character in Russian folklore, in Zhukovsky's Tsarevna-Marya is refined, presented as more feminine, more tender and modest. In the image of the hero, Ivan-Tsarevich, we are presented above all with a chivalrous knight of noble birth, characteristics not particularly typical of the Ivan-Tsarevich of folklore.

In his second tale—"Sleeping Beauty" (1831)—Zhukovsky showed that he was in fact capable of transferring a foreign story to a purely Russian setting. The "Sleeping Beauty" subject is not recorded in genuine Russian folklore. However, Zhukovsky painted it in vividly national colors (the description of the tsar and of his way of life, the appearance and costume of the beautiful tsarevna). Both the narrative style, replete with a certain "sly" humor, and the verse form (four-foot trochaic lines with masculine rhymes and marked accentuation) are close to the folklore style. Indeed, the verse form is almost identical with that of Pushkin's tales, "Tsar Saltan," "The Dead Tsarevna" ("O mertvoi Tsarevne"), and "The Golden Cock" ("O zolotom petushke").

From the point of view of sheer artistry, Zhukovsky's best tale in verse is also his last. This was "The Tale of Ivan-Tsarevich and the Gray Wolf" ("Skazka ob Ivane-Tsareviche i serom volke," 1845). Based on sources from Russian folklore, it is at the same time particularly complex from the point of view of inner meaning, since it has a hidden, biographical "stock-taking" significance for the author. The Russian folklore level is splendid for its specific imaginative power (the motif of the wonderful "firebird") and the very characteristic line of humor. One cannot help noticing that, in all of Zhukovsky's tales, the descriptions of court life and customs are more detailed and occupy more space than is usual in the folktale. Zhukovsky tells his story in a determinedly humorous tone. Nevertheless, the most amusing episodes at the end have their own, bitter meaning. The arrival of Gray Wolf, for instance, in a coach with the family arms emblazoned on the door showing a tail on a red background, and Gray Wolf at the end of the story described as teaching the royal children arithmetic and leaving a pile of manuscripts behind him when he dies—all this cannot fail to remind us of Zhukovsky.

Zhukovsky's tales are free of the dreaminess and high lyricism we have come to associate with his work in other genres. His poetic instinct evidently told him that here they would have been out of place. The remarkable "Tale of Ivan-Tsarevich," however, successfully combines three planes of thought: the folklore, the personal, and the general. Zhukovsky, who in his other works tended to linger on themes of particular importance to him, here skips lightly over them. And this "repetition," executed in quite another register, of all that has preceded, is deeply impressive.

In the descriptions of joyful meetings and fabulous feasts we catch a faint echo of Zhukovsky's "Homeric" tones; there are even a few compound epithets. The tsarevich's magic steed reminds us of his counterparts from the fantastic world of the ballads. In "The Twelve

Sleeping Maidens" there was a preview, as it were, of the enchanted kingdom of sleep. And the heroine's very name, Elena Prekrasnaya (Helen the Beautiful), has obvious Homeric associations.

A lyric poet *par excellence*, Zhukovsky's working life witnessed his steady progress from the lyric to the epic. It was likewise progress toward a wider and more balanced view of life, toward inner peace and wisdom.

Conclusion

ZHUKOVSKY's influence on contemporary Russian poetry and on the further development of Russian poetry was channeled in various directions. Like every great poet, he had his epigones who skimmed the surface of his work, imitating his "melancholy" themes and sentimental style. Zhukovsky's great service to literature, however, was his methodological influence. This went to fundamental questions of poetic thought and imagery. In his lyrics as in his epics, Zhukovsky always endeavored to make his poetry a vehicle for the expression of the spiritual life of man as an organic synthesis of the personal, the philosophical, and the social spheres of awareness. It was this objective that opened the way for the innovations and discoveries of future generations of Russian poets.

Zhukovsky's epic works, both original and translated, and particularly his ballads, revealed to Russian literature the possibility of creating local color outside the specific framework of Romanticism. Where poetic language was concerned, Zhukovsky elaborated a "conversational" syntax of the utmost importance for his immediate heir, Pushkin. In their transmutations these forms in themselves served to further the free expression of the author's own awareness of life through poetry.

Zhukovsky gave Russia examples of new meters that had never before been employed. Among other things, his poetry contains a remarkable wealth of trisyllabic meters, of which Pushkin, preferring to elaborate the iambic forms, made little or no use. Complex techniques of internal rhyming, free, noncanonical placing of the caesura, the first attempts at pause-substitution in trisyllabic meters—all these metrical riches were first made part of the Russian literary heritage by Zhukovsky. Also, the phonetic musicality of Zhukovsky's verse strongly influenced the poetry of the Russian Symbolists.

Zhukovsky stands at the very source of Russian Symbolism, occupying no less important a place in its genealogy than does the Symbolism of western Europe. The mystic conception of "two worlds," the symbolic quality of word images, not only in the poetry of Tyutchev and Fet, but also of Vladimir Solovev and even of Aleksandr Blok, still bear traces of their origin in the Romantic "philosophy" and poetry of Zhukovsky.

At the same time, Zhukovsky's poetry can by no means be said to have merged with the broad stream of poetry of the nineteenth and twentieth centuries. Even the greatest of those Russian poets (Pushkin, Tyutchev, Blok) who owe a considerable debt to Zhukovsky, do not so much overshadow as set off the unique quality of his poetic voice.

Zhukovsky is a poet of a specific range of themes and a specific intonation. His themes are usually sad, while his intonation is comforting. The integrity of Zhukovsky's poetic emotion and the concentrated intensity of his lyricism still make a deep impression upon his reader.

Notes and References

Foreword

1. M. V. Lomonosov, *Izbrannye proizvedeniia* (Moscow-Leningrad, 1965), pp. 286–87.
2. V. G. Belinsky, *Polnoe sobranie sochinenii* (Moscow-Leningrad, 1958), VII, 223. Further references to Belinsky's work will be to this edition.
3. V. A. Zhukovsky, *Polnoe sobranie sochinenii*, 12 vols. (St. Petersburg, 1902), IX, 123. Cited below as Zhukovsky, *Polnoe sobranie sochinenii*.

Chapter One

1. Zhukovsky, *Polnoe sobranie sochinenii*, XII, 131.
2. V. A. Zhukovsky, *Sobranie sochinenii v 4-kh tomakh*, 4 vols. (Moscow-Leningrad, 1959–60), I, 99. Cited below as Zhukovsky, *Sobranie sochinenii*.
3. Belinsky, VII, 139.
4. Zhukovsky, *Sobranie sochinenii*, IV, 491.
5. A. S. Pushkin, *Sobranie sochinenii*, 10 vols. (Moscow, 1962), IX, 224. Cited below as Pushkin, *Sobranie sochinenii*.
6. Letter to Aleksandr Turgenev of April 25, 1817, in Zhukovsky, *Polnoe sobranie sochinenii*, XII, 98.
7. *Russkaia starina*, no. 10 (1896), p. 32.
8. A. N. Veselovsky, *V. A. Zhukovsky: Poeziia chuvstva i serdechnogo voobrazheniia* (Petrograd, 1918), p. 49. Cited below as Veselovsky.
9. A. S. Pushkin, *Polnoe sobranie sochinenii*, 16 vols. (USSR Academy of Sciences, 1937–49), VI, 621. Cited below as Pushkin, *Polnoe sobranie sochinenii*.
10. Pushkin, *Sobranie sochinenii*, IX, 101.
11. Zhukovsky, *Polnoe sobranie sochinenii*, XII, 32.
12. Ibid., X, 138.
13. Ibid., XII, 39.
14. Ibid., p. 40.
15. Ibid., p. 41.

16. Ibid., p. 43.
17. K. K. Zeydlits, *Zhizn' i poeziia V. A. Zhukovskogo* (St. Petersburg, 1883), pp. 215–16.
18. Belinsky, VII, 199.

Chapter Two

1. Zhukovsky, *Polnoe sobranie sochinenii*, X, 81–88; Veselovsky, pp. 239–40.
2. G. A. Gukovsky, *Pushkin i russkie romantiki* (Moscow, 1965), pp. 42–43 ff.
3. Belinsky, VII, 215.
4. B. A. Larin, "O lirike kak raznovidnosti khudozhestvennoi rechi," *Russkaia rech'* (Leningrad), 1927.
5. N. A. Polevoy, *Ocherki russkoi literatury* (St. Petersburg, 1839), I, 115. Cited below as Polevoy, *Ocherki*.
6. B. M. Eykhenbaum, *Melodika russkogo liricheskogo stikha* (Petrograd, 1922), chapter on Zhukovsky.
7. The term is V. M. Zhirmunsky's. Cf. V. Zhirmunsky, "Zadachi poetiki," in *Voprosy teorii literatury* (Leningrad, 1928), pp. 39–43.
8. Zhukovsky, *Polnoe sobranie sochinenii*, X, 102.
9. N. L. Stepanov, *Lirika Pushkina* (Moscow, 1959), pp. 121–27. Cited below as Stepanov. See also L. Ya. Ginzburg, *O lirike* (Moscow-Leningrad, 1964), pp. 159–71. Cited below as Ginzburg.
10. Polevoy, *Orcherki*, p. 116.
11. Veselovsky, p. 107.
12. Pushkin, *Sobranie sochinenii*, IX, 162.
13. *Gedichte von Friedrich Schiller*, 2 vols. (Leipzig, 1801 and 1806), II, 19. In the text, following quotations from Schiller's verse, the reference is to this edition.

Chapter Three

1. V. V. Vinogradov, *Stil' Pushkina* (Moscow, 1941). Cited below as Vinogradov.
2. K. N. Batyushkov, *Polnoe sobranie stikhotvorenii* (Moscow-Leningrad, 1964), p. 173.
3. K. N. Batyushkov, *Sochineniia* (Leningrad, 1934), p. 399.
4. Zhukovsky, *Polnoe sobranie sochinenii*, XII, 128.
5. Belinsky, XII, 223.
6. K. F. Ryleev, *Stikhotvoreniia* (Leningrad, 1956), p. 105.
7. Ibid., p. 108.
8. Pushkin, *Sobranie sochinenii*, IX, 130.
9. Pushkin, *Polnoe sobranie sochinenii*, XI, 159.
10. For more detail, cf. Irina M. Semenko, *Poety pushkinskoi pory* (Moscow, 1970), pp. 285–88.

11. See *Poetry 1820–1830–kh godov* (Leningrad, 1961). Cf. also the introductory article by L. Ya. Ginzburg to *Russkaia lirika 1820–1830–kh godov*.

12. A. Blok, "Avtobiografiia," *Sochineniia v dvukh tomakh* (Moscow, 1955), II, 207.

Chapter Four

1. Veselovsky, p. 419.

2. *Russkii arkhiv*, 5 (1902), 145.

3. Vsevolod Cheshikhin, *Zhukovsky kak perevodchik Shillera* (Riga, 1895), p. 171.

Chapter Five

1. *The Works of Robert Southey* (Zwickau, 1820), vol. I, parts I–II. Quotations from Southey's verse in the text will be cited according to this edition. Here the quotation is from part II, p. 92.

2. Letter to A. I. Turgenev of October 20, 1814, in *Pis'ma Zhukovskogo k A. I. Turgenevu* (Moscow, 1895), p. 128.

3. Belinsky, VII, 167.

4. *"Prosto serdtse": Stikhi zarubezhnykh poetov v perevode Mariny Tsvetaevoi* (Moscow, 1967), pp. 88–95.

5. Walter Scott, *Ballads and Lyrical Pieces* (Edinburgh, 1806), p. 28. Page references given in the text to the poems of Walter Scott are to this edition, unless expressly stated otherwise.

6. Ludwig Uhland, *Gedichte* (Stuttgart and Tübingen, 1815), p. 264.

Chapter Six

1. Introductory article by B. V. Tomashevsky to K. N. Batyushkov, *Stikhotvoreniia* (Leningrad, 1948).

2. A letter of February, 1815, from K. N. Batyushkov to P. A. Vyazemsky, in *Russkaia literatura*, no. 1 (1970), p. 187.

Chapter Seven

1. A letter from P. A. Vyazemsky to Aleksandr Turgenev, dated October 7, 1819, in *Ostaf'evskii arkhiv*, I, 327.

2. Belinsky, VII, 209.

3. Pushkin, *Sobranie sochinenii*, IX, 78.

4. Zhukovsky, *Sobranie sochinenii*, IV, 659.

5. Ibid., pp. 659–60.

6. Zhukovsky, *Polone sobranie sochinenii*, X, 98–106.

7. A. N. Afanasev, *Narodnye russkie skazki* (Moscow, 1957), III, 382.

Selected Bibliography

1. Editions of Zhukovsky's Works in Russian

Sochineniia, ed. by P. Efremov. 6 vols. St. Petersburg, 1878.
Polnoe sobranie sochinenii, ed. by A. Arkhangelsky. 12 vols. St. Petersburg, 1902.
Stikhotvoreniia, ed. by Ts. Volpe. Leningrad, 1936.
Stikhotvoreniia, ed. by Ts. Volpe. 2 vols. Leningrad, 1939–40.
Stikhotvoreniia, ed. by N. V. Izmaylov. Leningrad, 1956.
Sobranie sochinenii v 4-kh tomakh. 4 vols. Moscow-Leningrad, 1959–60.
  Vol. I: Poetry. Edited by V. P. Petushov, with an introductory article by I. M. Semenko.
  Vol. II: Ballads, poems and tales. Edited by I. M. Semenko.
  Vol. III: The Maid of Orleans, fairytales and epics. Edited by N. V. Izmaylov.
  Vol. IV: The Odyssey, fiction and critical articles. Edited by I. D. Glikman.

2. Translations of Zhukovsky's Works into English

Bowring, John, trans. *Specimens of the Russian Poets*. 2 vols. London, 1821, 1823.

3. Scholarly Works on Zhukovsky in Russian

Belinsky, V. "Sochineniia Aleksandra Pushkina" (articles 2, 4, and 5), *Polnoe sobranie sochinenii*. vol. V. Moscow, 1955.
———. "Russkaia literatura v 1841 godu," Ibid., pp. 545–50.
Cheshikhin, V. *Zhukovsky kak perevodchik Shillera*. Riga, 1895.
Eykhenbaum, B. Chapter on Zhukovsky in *Melodika russkogo liricheskogo stikha*. Petrograd, 1922.
Gukovsky, G. *Pushkin i russkie romantiki*. Moscow, 1965.
Izmaylov, N. "V. A. Zhukovsky." In *Istoriia russkoi poezii*, pp. 237–65.
Rezanov, V. *Iz razyskanii o sochineniiakh V. A. Zhukovskogo*. 2 vols. St. Petersburg, 1906, 1916.
Sakulin, P. "M. A. Protasova-Moier po ee pis'mam." In *Izvestiia II otdeleniia Akademii nauk*, vol. XIII, book 1. St. Petersburg, 1907.

Semenko, I. "V. A. Zhukovsky." In Zhukovsky, *Sobranie sochinenii v 4-kh tomakh*, vol. I. Moscow-Leningrad, 1959.
———. "Pushkin i Zhukovsky." *Nauchnye doklady vysshei shkoly, filologicheskie nauki*, no. 4. (Moscow, 1964)
———. Chapter on Zhukovsky in *Poety pushkinskoi pory*. Moscow, 1970.
Shestakov, S. "Zhukovsky kak perevodchik Gomera." In *Chteniia v Obshchestve liubitelei russkoi slovesnosti*. Kazan', 1902.
Volpe, Ts. Introduction to Zhukovsky, *Stikhotvoreniia*. Leningrad, 1939.
———. "Zhukovsky." *Istoriia russkoi literatury* (Moscow-Leningrad), 5 (1941), 355–91.
Zaytsev, B. *Zhukovsky*. Paris, 1951.
Zeydlits, K. *Zhizn' i poeziia V. A. Zhukovskogo*. St. Petersburg, 1883.

4.   Scholarly Works on Zhukovsky in Other Languages
Ellis (Kobilinsky, L.). *W. A. Joukowski, seine Persönlichkeit, sein Leben und sein Werk*. Paderborn, 1933.
Ehrhard, M. *V. A. Joukovski et le préromantisme russe*. Paris, 1938.
Gerhardt, D. *Vergangene Gegenwärtigkeiten*. Göttingen, 1966.
Ober, K. H., and W. U. Ober, "Žukovskij's First Translation of Gray's 'Elegy'," *Slavic and East European Journal*, vol. X, No. 2 (Summer 1966), pp. 167–172.
———. "Žukovskij's Early Translations of the Ballads of Robert Southey," *ibid.*, vol. IX, No. 2 (Summer 1965), pp. 181–190.

Index